MW01127796

Symbols of Faith and the Miracles of God

Keith G. Allen

Wells of Water Publishing

Copyright © 2006 by Wells of Water Publishing

Keith G. Allen. All rights reserved. All
quotations in this book are divinely inspired and
therefore written permission must be obtained
from the publisher to use or reproduce any part
of this book, except for brief quotation in critical
reviews or articles.

Published in Windsor Mill, Maryland by Wells of
Water and distributed in the United States by
Wells of Water, Post Office Box 47335, Windsor
Mill, Maryland 21244,
www.Roshanne.org

Printed in the United States of America

"Scripture quotations taken from the Amplified®
Bible, Copyright © 1954, 1958, 1962, 1964, 1965,
1987 by The Lockman Foundation Used by
permission." (www.Lockman.org)

ISBN: 978-0-9789462-0-3
Library of Congress Control Number:
2006939689
Allen, Keith G.
Symbols of Faith and the Miracles of God

Dedication

This book is dedicated to my daughter Talisa Howlett who died from cancer October 27, 2005. Some of the proceeds from this book will help defray college expenses for her children.

Acknowledgements

Thanks to my family for their encouragement to pursue writing this book. Thanks to my wife Gloria for her inspiration. Thanks to my daughter Deitre for proofreading the script in order to have the book presented well. Thanks to my daughter and son Michelle and Michael for their long distance encouragement. Also to Jodi my youngest daughter, for her inspiration to continue. A special thanks to my daughter Roshanne who literally "pushed" me to write. Roshanne retyped and edited the script several times. She had the charge of publishing and marketing the book.

A special thanks to Judith Wright who was the original typist. To Adrianne Moore who was one of the original editors and all of my grandchildren for being there when I needed them.
A special thanks to my Rehoboth church family who constantly prayed for me.

Foreword

Symbols of Faith and the Miracles of God is indeed a refreshing break from the redundant "prosperity" message books of today. I praise God that in times like these He continues to use men, such as Bishop Keith George Allen, to help unlock the mysteries of His word. I am especially thankful that we still have men who not only hear and obey the word of the Lord, but also are mindful to make this knowledge available and specifically directing it to those who are interested in a deeper understanding of the mysteries of God.

In these challenging times when people are looking for direction in their lives, and searching for answers on how to actuate miracles such as was demonstrated in the days of old; Symbols of Faith and the Miracles of God will serve as a "Word-evidenced" road map for years to come.

As you begin to read, think it not strange that each chapter will stir up a longing and thirst within you to move beyond the routine surface knowledge of God and tap into a spiritual and divine level that only can be attained through unadulterated truth as presented in this book.

Truly God has inspired Bishop Allen as he has written—from a Biblical perspective—detailed explanations of 'what,' 'in whom', and 'why' we believe what we believe. A much-needed substantive book, Symbols of Faith and the Miracles of God is a must-read for every faith leader and layperson also—regardless of his or her denominational affiliation.

It has blessed my inner man and if applied to your heart, I am sure it will bless yours too!

Mrs. Vivian Berryhill,
President and Founder of the National Coalition of Pastors' Spouses
New Philadelphia Baptist Church-Memphis, TN
Reverend Chester Berryhill, Jr., Senior Pastor

Table of Content

"Don't remind me of yesterday; for today is too exciting and tomorrow holds so much promise!"

Pastor Keith G. Allen

Symbols of Faith and the Miracles of God

Introduction:

Often times we view God in a one-dimensional manner. That is, we see God using one particular method to accomplish a task; therefore all tasks are brought about by that method. However, God is a God that works in different ways. Hebrews illustrates this point. "In many separate revelations and in different ways God spoke of old to our forefathers in and by the prophets." Here, God Himself is telling us that He is not one-dimensional. He has many facets. When we view God one-dimensionally, we may miss the blessings or the miracles that God has for us, because we are *not* looking for God to work in a way that is unfamiliar to us. In exploring the symbols used by God in scripture to effect mighty miracles, I hope to enlighten the reader to employ these methods, and if God so chooses, He will cause you to receive your own miracle.

Webster's dictionary defines symbol as "something that stands for something else: something concrete that represents or suggest another thing that cannot in itself be pictured."

1

Faith is belief in the word of God, and the word of God has the power to effect that which is spoken. If you are a Bible scholar, you will be familiar with many of these symbols, but you may not have thought God could use similar symbols to bless you. If you are a "budding" Bible scholar, read with anticipation to find the God of symbols and miracles.

CHAPTER ONE

"Faith is the substance of things hoped for, the evidence of things not seen."
Hebrews 11:1

The Burning Bush

Moses is the man through whom God predetermined to deliver the Israelites out of Egypt by great miracles, signs, and wonders. Now Moses kept the flock of Jethro his father-in-law, a priest of Midian: and he took the flock to the backside of the desert, and came to the mountain of God, called Horeb. Moreover, the angel of the Lord appeared unto him in a flame of fire out of the midst of a bush: and he looked, and behold, the bush burned with fire, and the bush was not consumed. Moses said, "I will now turn aside, and see this great sight, why the bush is not burnt." When the Lord saw that he turned aside to see, God called unto him out of the midst of the bush, and said, "Moses, Moses," and he said, "Here am I."[1]

The symbol of the burning bush illustrates a great miracle, not a miracle for Moses, but a miracle for God to establish and build Moses' faith. "But without faith it is impossible to please God."[2]

We are familiar with seeing brush fires, forest fires and other fires. Fires with which we are

acquainted are consuming fires; fires that burn rapidly,
even demolishing great houses that are in its path.
Moses was most likely knowledgeable about types of
fires and how they burn.

Visualize if you will, Moses' amazement when
he sees this fire that is not consuming. This fire grabs
the attention of Moses. God will use attention- getting
symbols also to draw us into His "holy ground" where
He can speak to us and show us His power.

God was getting ready to use Moses in a great
miraculous way – was Moses ready? No!! God
informed Moses that He was assigning him to go back
to Egypt to deliver His people. Moses began to make
excuses. "And Moses said unto God, 'Who am I, that I
should go unto Pharaoh, and that I should bring forth
the children of Israel out of Egypt?' Moses' second
excuse was, "But, behold, they will not believe me, nor
hearken unto my voice: for they will say the Lord hath
not appeared unto thee.' Moses continued with his
third excuse, "O my Lord, I am not eloquent, neither
heretofore, nor since thou hast spoken unto thy
servant: but I am slow of speech, and of a slow
tongue."[3] Moses' last line of defense in establishing his
un-readiness to God is found in Exodus 4:13. Moses
said to God, "O my Lord, send, I pray thee, by the

hand of him whom thou wilt send." Oh, the wonderful mercies of God. The only drawback: Moses did not know what was ahead. Moses did not know the power that was about to be unleashed through him. Moses saw the burning bush-a symbol. He heard the voice (of God) speaking to him. The word of God says "we walk by faith and not by sight."[4] God sometimes chooses not to reveal to us the future. There is a very good reason for this: If God shows us the good, He would also show us the bad. If God shows us the power, He would also show us the persecution.

Knowing our propensity to worry or withdraw from experiences that are negative, and to sorrow over things that are hurtful, such as death; we certainly would not go forward at the command of God. For example, if God was to show you that He is going to use you in mighty miracles, signs and wonders, and in the midst of that great work you would be persecuted, ostracized, become hungry and thirsty with no food or water in sight, would you leave your good job? Alternatively, would you leave your thriving pastorate, and give up your secured bank account to go where you did not know where you are going? I dare say most people would say that is not God talking. "God would not take me from a secured environment to an experience of that nature." Given the climate of prosperity preaching today, I do not believe I am far off base. Nevertheless, that is the very environment that Moses was sent. Consider the fact that Moses was seeing a great phenomenon and was still making excuses.

What if God would show him all that would befall him? I think Moses would have said to the burning bush, "See you later bush."

So then, I believe there are two reasons for God not always revealing our future: One, we must walk by faith and not by sight; Two, we would not appreciate the negatives in our future. Therefore, we would not go forward into the great miracles of God.

Walking by faith and cooperating with God are two prerequisites necessary to experience miracles manifested in and through us. Most miracles are realized only when we work with God. God can be very convincing when He chooses us to work with Him to accomplish His divine purpose as He was with Moses. No excuses by Moses would deter God from using him to accomplish His great purpose. It is amazing that God revealed Himself to Moses in such a great symbol of His power and signs, and yet Moses was making excuses to God showing why he was not qualified as a vessel used of God. Of course, the Lord would not listen to any of Moses' excuses. Neither will the Lord listen to our excuses because the power is not of men but of God.

To experience God's miracles we must be able to believe in God and recognize His faith symbols. So many times, we think that we must be completely ready when God calls us. On the other hand, we prejudge someone whom God has called when we see them moving towards their burning bush. We tend to say, "God cannot use you; you are not ready." The one that God has called is caught in the middle of two challenges. He is caught, on one hand, with his fears. On the other hand, he has verbal blocks of those whom (without fear) tell him: "You cannot be used of God; you are not ready." Moses was blessed in that he was in the desert alone. There was no one to say, "Moses, you cannot go near the bush that is burning, but not consumed." You must realize that God may not reveal himself to you in a literal burning bush as he did Moses. Child of God, the time is now to be ready to recognize the faith building experience that God is drawing you. Whatever means God uses to draw your attention to Him will be just as dramatic as the burning bush. You, however, must have enough faith to draw closer.

My burning bush was the death of a great teacher, preacher, and man of God: Bishop Earl Fisher. At his home-going service, the spirit of the Lord spoke to me and said, "Resign your job and go into full time ministry." Was I ready? No! I had a good, secure, stable job working with a notable Fortune 500 corporation. I had a wife and children to support; I did not have excess money in the bank. However, my burning bush was so compelling that I said, "Yes" to God. Thank God!

Have there been difficult years? Yes. Have there been struggles? Yes. I truly believe that if I had not said yes to that burning bush experience, I would not be pastoring at the church I am today. Pastoring the church was definitely a miracle, and without question, the workings of God Almighty.

Notwithstanding, God used man to effect His will, as is His standard operating procedure. Would I have resigned my job if God had shown me all the trials and tribulations that I have gone through? Hindsight will say yes, but what really would my response have been? What do you think your response would have been without hindsight?

Remember, the miracle that is in the symbol of the burning bush is the building of a greater faith to do a superior work with and for God. Bishop Fisher was my symbol. At the end of his days, he suffered a very long time with a sickness that eventually caused his death. The doctor wanted to amputate his foot, but Bishop Fisher said, "No." He suffered to the very end with his faith intact. To do a superior work for God we must know God in a better way. We must be acquainted with His better promises.

Moses and Saul of Tarsus

Both Moses and Saul were ordained by God to do a greater work. Like Moses, Saul, (also named Paul) was blinded by a light from heaven. The Lord called out to him, "Saul, Saul, why persecutest thou me?"[5] Like Moses, Saul experienced a bright light. Both men had their burning bush experience. Let us look at the contrasting manner of their call. Both men had faith in God but needed a greater faith to do the work. Moses ran away from Pharaoh's sword because of his defense of God's people. Saul was persecuting God's people. In each case God spoke first, and called them by their names, "Moses, Moses," and "Saul, Saul"[6]

In each of these cases, God called their names twice. Is it significant that God called their names twice? Of course it is. God wanted their instant attention. Has anyone ever called your name once and you sort of heard, but really didn't pay attention? God wanted their immediate attention. When God has a greater work for us, his call is dramatic.

We do not define what we do for God. God defines what we will do for him. To do a work, we must know God in a better way. Moses asked God, "What name should I use to tell the Israelites that you sent me?"[7] "I Am," was the reply. Saul asked God, "Who art thou Lord?" "I Am Jesus,"[8] was the answer. Note that Jesus identified Himself as the "I AM" in the New Testament (John 8:58). It is of utmost importance to know God's name. Moses and Saul knew this. Both men knew that the power is in the name. Both men came to know God more intimately in His power. They were ready to heed the call of God. Both men experienced the mighty power of God in signs, wonders, and miracles, as we shall see in detail in the following chapters.

CHAPTER TWO

"Faith is the substance of things hoped for, the evidence of things not seen."
Hebrews 11:1

The Rod of Moses

Moses became a great symbol of faith for God's manifestation of great miracles. God outlined to Moses the scope of the work and the deliverance of the Israelites from Egypt. Moses said to God, "The people will not believe me." God said to Moses, "What is in your hand Moses?" "A rod,"[9] God shifted the focus symbol of the burning bush from Himself to Moses' rod as the faith symbol. What is God teaching from this paradigm shift? God is teaching that He will use what we own, although it may appear very insignificant. Certainly, a rod or stick could be designated as insignificant.

More often than not, what we have is what God wants to use. It could be the simplest of things that no one, but God would think of using. For example, when God wanted to sustain the prophet Elijah through the famine, he sent him to a very poor widow woman (1Kings 17). We will deal with her in chapter six. What is in your hand that God can use? Let us call this symbol of faith a resource. The meal and oil were the widow's resource. Your resource could be your time. Are you giving God enough of your time for Him to work your miracle? Another resource could be your tithes (10% of your increase) and your offerings to God. One has to have faith in order to give sacrificially. Tithe and offerings can become a symbol of faith at the time when you are in great need financially. Conflict will develop in your mind whether to give or not to give. Always make the decision to give so that God can use your symbol to create your miracle.

A sister, who was a member of our church, was faithful in giving her tithes and offerings. The time came when her job was downsizing. She was on the list to be laid-off. We prayed and reminded God that she was faithful in presenting to Him her symbol of faith, tithes, and offerings. She received her miracle and yet on the same job receiving promotions and raises. This book has been written several years after she was on the list to be laid-off.

As stated, God used the burning bush that was not consumed to attract Moses' attention. Whatever symbol God uses to attract your attention, eventually He will say to you, "What is in your hand?" God saw what Moses had in his hand, but he wanted a response from Moses. God will not use us until we respond to

12

Him. "I beseech you therefore brethren, by the mercies of God, that ye present your bodies as a living sacrifice, wholly acceptable unto God, which is your reasonable service."[10] This is a very good place to start. It takes great faith to give our total being as a symbol of faith to God. When we do, God anoints us with power to affect miracles-This is a show of faith. Let yourself be used of God mightily.

God said to Moses, cast the rod that is in your hand to the ground. Moses, "I am getting ready to use you and I am not giving you anything but faith, faith to empower what you already have and I will anoint what you have, to manifest my power to show miracles." Moses now had demonstrated obedience by throwing the rod to the ground. I wonder if it flashed through Moses' mind, "Maybe God wants me to throw this simple rod away. There is no use for it any longer. God is getting ready to use me mightily." If Moses thought that, he did not have time to dwell on it. Immediately the rod became a serpent. Has God ever worked in your life so fast that you did not have time to think? The phenomenon was so great that it scared Moses. Moses began to run from his own rod because it was no longer a rod. History tells us that the Pharaohs of Egypt used the serpent as a symbol of power and royalty, therefore, Moses quite certainly was well aware of this symbol of power. I believe God was saying to Moses, "Moses, I am sending you to Pharaoh, and I am giving you power over Pharaoh's power. I am anointing what you have. I am empowering what you have. Do not fear." To do the greater work for God-situations will arise that are more powerful than one could expect. God will anoint and empower you to do what is necessary. One should not become fearful, however. God told Moses to pick up the serpent by its tail. Notice how specific God is in Exodus Chapter 4:1-2:

> And Moses answered and said, "But, behold, they will not believe me, nor hearken unto my voice: For they will say, The LORD hath not appeared unto thee." And the LORD said unto him, What is that in thine hand?" And he said A rod. And He said, Cast it on the ground. And he cast it on the ground, and it became a serpent; and Moses fled from before it.

We must also obey implicitly. We must follow God's instruction to the letter. Moses picked up the serpent by its tail, just as God ordered, and it became a rod again. Moses' rod had become a symbol of faith to show forth the miracles of God.

The Leprous Hand

He gave Moses symbols of faith to give to the
people so that they could believe.

> *And the LORD said unto Moses, Put forth thine
> hand, and take it by the tail. And he put forth his
> hand, and caught it, and it became a rod in his hand:
> That they may believe that the LORD God of their
> fathers, the God of Abraham, the God of Isaac, and the
> God of Jacob, hath appeared unto thee. And the
> LORD said furthermore unto him, Put now thine hand
> into thy bosom. And he put his hand into his bosom:
> and when he took it out, behold, his hand was leprous as
> snow. And he said, Put thine hand into thy bosom
> again. And he put his hand into his bosom again; and
> plucked it out of his bosom, and, behold, it was turned
> again as his other flesh. And it shall come to pass, if
> they will not believe thee, neither hearken to the voice of
> the first sign, that they will believe the voice of the latter
> sign.*[11]

What a living God, what a merciful God, what a
great Savior!   The Lord God could have said; "Moses
your faith has now been magnified through the
experience of the burning bush. Now go and tell my
people." God knew that the people's faith needed to
be increased. So, what did God do? What is our God

saying to us? For the greater works, both the minister and the people need their faith increased.

God provides symbols for the minister and gives symbol to the people. Does God work with symbols today? Yes, He does. In later chapters, we will explore New Testament symbols. Moses' rod has now become a powerful symbol of faith. "And it shall come to pass, if they will not believe thee, neither hearken to the voice of the first sign, and then they will believe the voice of the latter sign."[12] Notice the rod has now become a voice (according to Romans 10:17). "Faith comes by hearing the word of God."[13] "*And Moses and Aaron went and gathered together all the elders of the children of Israel. And Aaron spake all the words which the Lord had spoken unto Moses, and did the sign in the sight of the people. And the people believed.*"[14]

A symbol creates faith. Faith creates the miracles of God. Study the great miracles the rod of faith was able to manifest.

Miracle to Defeat the Enemy and the Enemy's gods
God further instructs Moses:

"*When Pharaoh says to you prove your authority by a miracle then shall thou say unto Aaron, take thy rod and cast it before Pharaoh and it shall become a serpent. Then Pharaoh also called the wise men and the sorcerers. Now the magicians of*

16

Egypt, they also did as like manner with their enchantments.
For they cast down every man his rod, and they became serpents.
But Aaron's rod swallowed up their rod.[15]

Is not God the same today as He was then?
Should we not believe God that He uses symbols of
faith today? There are times your situations and
conditions will get worse. The enemy's symbols will
out-number your symbol. Nevertheless, your symbol is
a symbol of faith and it has the anointing. It will
overpower all unbelief, and you will have your miracle.
The ten plagues of Egypt were brought about by using
the rod of faith. This is called wearing down the enemy
for the kill. The rod of faith brings deliverance to
God's people and death to their enemies.[16] The rod
divides the water, and the rod brings the water back
together.[17]

Pharaoh and his army were swiftly chasing the
Israelites. However, they were blind---eyes wide open,
but blind. The world does not understand this
blindness. Pharaoh must have forgotten that God
orchestrated the ten plagues, and Moses' rod had
brought about the victory each time. Nevertheless,
Pharaoh was blind and his heart hardened toward God.
This type of blindness produces actions that are
detrimental to the blind. The individual that is

spiritually blind cannot discern the workings of God, although they are out in the open.

The water of the sea was backed up and became a wall on either side, while the earth between became dry ground for the Israelites to travel across. Pharaoh's only intention was to bring the Israelites back into captivity and slavery. The enemy's desire is to bring us back into bondage. The enemy cannot see the wall of protection surrounding God's people. The angel of the Lord encampeth round about them that fear Him and delivereth them (Psalm 34:7). Pharaoh's rage pushed him to pursue the Israelites only to find that the dry ground that the Israelites walked on suddenly became soggy.

Moses' symbol of faith, the rod, was able to produce another great miracle. As Moses stretched his rod over the sea, the waters returned to their original flow and drowned the Egyptians. The path that brought deliverance to Israel brought destruction to Egypt. Faith will allow us to see clearly God's victory, although surrounded by the enemy. "The Egyptians that you see today, you will see no more forever" (Exodus 14:13). Sometime we, as saints and believers in God Almighty, do not come to understand that God will allow an enemy to be completely destroyed, although there are many enemies in front of us that God will either protect us from or destroy for us. Our victories and our peace are both permanent and temporary. They are permanent in that through faith we always have the victory.[18] However, we must cross Jordan, each battle has to be fought, and each victory has to be won. Beloved, our God is able to deliver us. Look for your symbol.

CHAPTER THREE

"Faith is the substance of things hoped for, the evidence of things not seen."
Hebrews 11:1

Bitter and Sweet Water

It is interesting to note that when Israel crossed the Red Sea, the first water that they came to was bitter. How many times after great victories or just the vicissitudes of life, do we face bitterness? Some experiences are distasteful. Do we like knowing that the Israelites forgot the great victory of crossing the Red Sea and began to complain instead of giving God praise and thanks, and worshiping him for his goodness? The people complained in the city of Mara to Moses, "We have not water to drink" (Exodus 15:24).

Do not limit God to one method of performing miracles. Moses still had the rod of God. But God told Moses to use another piece of wood and throw the wood into the water. When he did, the water became sweet.[19] The wood became a symbol of faith. Without the wood, the water would not be healed. Moses had to learn God's way of working. His rod had been the main symbol. Now God wants to use something else. When the wood was thrown into the water, the water

was healed and made sweet. The Israelites had enough to drink. The Lord God performed this miracle to teach the Israelites the lesson that He is the God that heals. I am the Lord that heals you and if you keep my commandments, I will not put on you the diseases that I put on the Egyptians. God said to the Israelites:

"If thou wilt diligently hearken to the voice of the Lord thy God, and wilt do that which is right in His sight, and wilt give ear to His commandments, and keep all His statutes, I will put none of these diseases upon thee, which I have brought upon the Egyptians: for I am the Lord that healeth thee."[20]

In our faith journey, there will be seasons of bitterness. What should we do during the season of bitterness? According to the Lord God Almighty, we should continually give Him thanks, worship, and praise. "In every thing give thanks: for this is the will of God in Christ Jesus concerning you."[21]

I went through a season of bitterness, probably the greatest time of severe testing in my life. The church was greatly affected. Some members left the church. Those that remained were in a quandary. Through it all, I preached the word of God. I believed God would deliver us, and He did.

The city of Mara was not the final destination of the Israelites. A land flowing with milk and honey was their inheritance. Your season of bitterness will pass. Worship God, give Him thanks and praise. The Israelites passed Mara, but they failed their test. They murmured against their leader, Moses. There is one thing that God takes very seriously; His people resisting the leader that He chooses. Disrespecting His leader is always very displeasing to God; but God is very merciful. He heard the prayer of Moses, healed the waters of Mara, and allowed the Israelites to continue their journey.

The Israelites came to Elim, a place of blessings. Elim had twelve wells of water and seventy palm trees (Exodus 15:27). Water represents, or is a symbol of, the Holy Spirit. The twelve wells of water are prophetic of the future outpouring of the Holy Ghost upon the twelve tribes of Israel (Ezekiel 38, Revelation 7). The seventy palm trees spoke prophetically to Israel as well. Exodus chapter 24 records Moses choosing seventy elders to meet with God. The palm tree is also symbolic of stability and permanence.

Over time, Israel had experienced many changes. They were exiled, restored several times, their land, and the people had been decimated; yet today they remain a people united worldwide and believing in the one true God Jehovah. No other nation under heaven except for the Israelites could endure exile for thousands of years, maintain their identity, return unto their own land, (and) become a nation again with their original language. No one could accomplish this great miracle but Jehovah, God Himself. Truly, Israel is like the palm tree. Psalm 92:12 says:

> *"The righteous shall flourish like the palm tree: he shall grow like a cedar in Lebanon."*

The first city that Israel conquered after the crossing of Jordan was Jericho, the city of palm trees. So then, God revealed to Israel His present and future blessings by leading them to the camp at Elim. Elim had the prophetic symbols of faith: twelve wells of water and seventy palm trees. Israel is yet enjoying the miracles and blessings of Elim and will continue to do so into the future.

How unfortunate it is that the Israelites could not visualize all these blessings while they were at the City of Mara. Only their present situation at Mara was in their vision. They forgot the symbols of faith that produced great miracles while in Egypt. However, the great mercies of God and His covenant promises to Abraham, Isaac and Jacob caused Israel to forge ahead.

Dear Reader, while you are reading this book if you are going through a season of bitterness, be not discouraged; give God thanks. You will pass Mara and arrive at Elim, your place of blessings. Some people have dreams and visions. If you have a dream or vision of palm trees, know that God is blessing you right now and your blessings will continue into the future.

Wilderness Experiences

In the wilderness, God performed great wonders, miracles, and showed the Israelites wonderful signs. The rod of God became prominent in its use. When the Israelites had no water, God told Moses to strike the rock with the rod and water came from the rock. There are times when God works miracles independently of us. He sent the miracle of quail and manna for the people to eat. No symbol of faith was needed. Moses' faith was not needed and the people's faith was not needed, God just worked. God will work for us in like manner, as we walk by faith.

In the early 70's, there was a great earthquake in California; this earthquake caused massive damage to the infrastructure of many buildings, including our house. Of course, I did not know how to access those monies. I was not knowledgeable in the ways the various Federal agencies worked. I did not have the monies to repair my house readily accessible. At the same time, the job was transferring me to another city. The Lord miraculously sent someone to give the information, so the house could be repaired. Since we had to move to another city, we put our house up for sale. We had a buyer, however, the transaction was not completed prior to our moving. I thought of myself as helping the buyer by having him move in before the settlement. What he did was move in and never went to settlement. Nevertheless, look what God did; He worked a miracle independent of our participation. The buyer had to pay for all the expensive and expansive repairs to the house that we had contracted to a contractor. I call that God working a great miracle on our behalf.

The Israelites went from bitter water to no water at all; God told Moses to strike the rock with the symbol of faith, the rod of God, which was Moses' rod. Miraculously water came in abundance.[22]

Revelation of the Ark

The Ark became one of the most powerful symbols of faith. I will further address the revelation of the Ark in more detail in chapter four. Israel is coming out of an idolatrous worship environment. God now begins to establish His true worship; He gives Moses the Law. He instructs him to build the tabernacle. The focal point of worship is the Ark, a small box. In the box is the presence of God, revealed by a light called the Shikenah Glory. God is now decreasing the use of Moses' Rod. God does not intend for us to rely on only one method to see his works.

God is a multi-dimensional God. He works in many ways by various means and symbols.[23] In many separate revelations, each of which set forth a portion of the truth in different ways, God spoke of old to our forefathers in and by the prophets (Hebrew 1:1). To often when God works in a particular way with us, we take that to be the only way that God works. Again, being in the desert, traveling from place to place, water becomes a problem. As was the custom of the people when trials came, they murmured and complained instead of believing God (Numbers 20).

Moses and Aaron go to the tabernacle to worship; there is a valuable lesson here. Many people say, "I can worship wherever I am; at my home, at work or anywhere I am." That is true. People can and should worship anywhere. However, God has mandated that His people congregate to worship at a prescribed location for corporate worship, praise and thanksgiving. The type of church that I would recommend is an apostolic church that teaches repentance and water baptism in the Name of Jesus Christ with the infilling of the Holy Ghost (Acts 2:38). God spoke to Moses and Aaron after they entered the tabernacle to worship. God speaks to us when we are in corporate worship in a manner that He does not speak to His people outside of corporate worship. God told Moses and Aaron in the Tabernacle to take the rod, gather the people together, and speak to the rock before their eyes. Let them see what God can do. Water will again come from the rock.

Remember the first experience of water flowing from the rock? Did the Israelites forget this great miracle? How often do we forget what God does for us in the past? When we come to a difficult place of need, faith is not present to produce works for a victorious outcome for us to enjoy. In the first scenario, God said to Moses, "Take the rod." Now he took the rod. In the second scenario, God said, "Take the Elders." Now He says take the entire congregation. In the third scenario, God said, "Strike the rock." Now God says, "Speak to the rock." What is the lesson here? We must listen to God very carefully. The change in instruction may be ever so minor, but it is very important to God. Moses followed God's instructions, except in one area. Moses in anger struck the rock instead of speaking to the rock. Yes, the water sprang from the rock because Moses had such a close relationship with God. God honored Moses and caused the water to spring forth from the rock even though Moses disobeyed God. Was God pleased? No!! God was not pleased with Moses. "You failed to sanctify me in the eyes of the people," God said.

How many times does the Lord God bless us when we did not do things perfectly; but because we had a pure heart before him? As a chorus states, "He keeps right on blessing me." Should we not praise God for his great mercy continually? Yes, we should. This was the last time the symbol of faith; the rod was used. It is to our advantage and benefit to follow God's instructions to the letter.

God was moving on. However, Moses was not ready to move on to a higher level of faith. How many times does God want to take us to a higher level of faith in Him and we do the opposite or do something that we know has proven record of accomplishment? Speak to the rock was God's instruction. Moses allowed the unbelief of the people to deter him. Saints and friends of God, we cannot afford to let other people's unbelief hinder our blessings. Moses spoke to the rock. Jesus teaches this principle of speaking things into existence in the New Testament. "You shall have what you say. For verily I say unto you, that whosoever shall say unto this mountain, be thou removed, and be thou cast into the sea; and shall not doubt in his heart, but shall believe that those things that he says shall come to pass, he shall have whatsoever he says."[24] Speak to the rock, God commanded Moses. Moses struck the rock. Moses had not sanctified God before the people, so he could only view, not possess, or go over to the Promised Land.

The Ark: The New Symbol of Faith

The rod of God is now replaced by a new symbol of faith; the Ark of the Covenant. The Ark of the Covenant was a visual symbol of God's presence. It symbolized that God was always with the Israelites. The Ark contained an area that was called the Mercy Seat. Above the Mercy Seat was a light that shone, this light was called the Shikenah Glory. The Israelites knew that the light was a representation of God. God was now visible, available and the leader as another symbol of faith. Now the Israelites were able to approach the Mercy Seat to obtain mercy by God. The rod of God was associated with the pillar of cloud that led the Israelites by day and night, (at which time turned into fire). Now the Israelites are ready to possess the land and this will call for a new level of faith.

God instructed Moses to place three items in the Ark: the rod of Aaron that budded, the Ten Commandments, and a pot filled with manna. Remember the Shikenah Glory is in the Ark. The Israelites had wandered in the wilderness for forty years and after that Moses died and God buried him. Now was the time to cross over the river Jordan into the Promised Land. God chose Joshua to be the new leader and said to Joshua, "As I was with Moses, so I will be with you" (Joshua 3:7). When a leader dies, God wants the new leader to take the people to a higher level of faith.

In the exodus from Egypt, Israel had to cross the Red Sea. To go into the Promised Land they had to cross the river Jordan. The Ark, the new symbol of faith, had to be carried on the shoulders of the priests in front of the people. God commanded Joshua to march the people across the river to the other side. There was no rod to stretch across the water, and the priest had to bear the Ark. They could not stretch the

Ark over the water. The priests' feet had to step into the water.

I believe it took a greater faith for the priests to step into the waters than for Moses to stretch the rod over the water. It was not until the four priests, which carried the Ark, by faith placed their feet into the water. Thereafter, the waters parted for the Israelites to walk over on dry ground. They were commanded to step into the water – great faith was needed. Prior, God told Moses to stretch his rod *over* the water, but now they must step *into* the water and God went before them. As soon as the feet of the priests bearing the Ark touched the water, it was divided. The Israelites marched over on dry ground with Moses as the enemy pursued, however, the enemy was destroyed by God. With Joshua, the enemy had to be defeated by the people. There are times when God will defeat the enemy for us, but there are times when God expects us to defeat the enemy.

Ephesians 4:12 states:

That we wrestle not against flesh and blood but against principalities, against powers, against the ruler of the darkness of this world, against spiritual wickedness in high places.

Israel's enemy was natural. The church's enemy is spiritual. Look at the great symbols of faith found in Ephesians chapter 4 verses 13-18:

1. Loins girt about with truth
2. The breastplate of righteousness
3. The feet with the gospel shoes
4. Shield of faith
5. Helmet of salvation
6. Sword of the spirit; the word of God.

With these symbols of faith at our disposal, no enemy will be able to stand before us. We have already crossed Jordan. Let us possess the land.

Enemies that we must defeat are the lust of the flesh, the lust of the eyes and the pride of life. Lust and pride are strong emotions that must be defeated and conquer. There is one enemy that we all must conquer, that we have no power over, and that enemy is death. But, thanks be to God, our Lord Jesus Christ through his death, burial and resurrection, has conquered death for us. Through His life, we will possess the New Jerusalem, our heavenly home. We will possess mansions that are prepared for us. Hallelujah!

CHAPTER FOUR

"Faith is the substance of things hoped for, the evidence of things not seen."
Hebrews 11:1

The Revelation of the Ark:
Symbols of Remembrance

The importance of the Ark of the Covenant (also known as the Ark of the Lord) is the spiritual development of the Israelites and the spiritual implications to the church cannot be overstated. The Ark rested in what is called the "holy of holies" or the "most holy place" in the tabernacle and subsequently in the temple. The only person that was allowed to enter the most holy place was the high priest. He could only go in once per year, on the specific Day of Atonement. The spiritual application for the church is that when Jesus the Lamb of God was slain, the veil of the temple was torn in two. Jesus, our great high priest, entered in leading the way for us to come boldly to the throne of grace to obtain mercy and find grace to help us in the time of need.[25] Oh, what marvelous grace the Lord has given to us under the new covenant.

The Ark was primarily made of two things, Shittim wood and gold (Exodus 37:1-2), which are very durable materials. The wood is a symbol of man and gold is the symbol of God's authority. The pure gold

33

completely covers the wood so that none of the wood is to be seen. Thus, the authority or glory of God will eventually cover completely the humanity of man, so that only God will be seen. Hallelujah!!! This beloved, is our glorious hope. The priest would carry the Ark, the symbol of God's presence, and go before the congregation. God's presence insured victory for the people. The priests bearing the Ark stepped into the waters of the Jordan River, the waters parted and the children of Israel crossed over to the Promised Land on dry ground (Joshua chapter 3).

We who are born of God do not carry God's presence on the outside. We have Him by His spirit on the inside. Everywhere the sole of our feet treads we have the victory. "For as many as are led by the spirit of God, they are the sons of God" (Romans 8:14), representing our Lord Jesus Christ everywhere. There are many lessons to be learned from the greatest of symbols of faith. One could write a book alone on the Ark of the Covenant and how the Israelites' experienced great miracles as a result. Therefore, I will concentrate the rest of this lesson on the three symbols that were placed in the Ark that I would call the symbols of faith for remembrance.

God instructed Moses to place three items inside the Ark of the Covenant of the Lord. The two tables of stone on which were written the Ten Commandments, a pot of manna and Aaron's rod that budded. Let us consider the reasons why and the purpose for putting these items in the Ark. The first item that we will examine is the two tables of stone.

Symbol of faith for remembrance: the Ten Commandments.

God wrote the Ten Commandments with His fingers for Moses upon Mount Sinai.[26] These basic laws of the Kingdom of God were given to govern His people. The first and foremost of these commandments are, "Hear O Israel: the Lord our God is one Lord."[27] Imagine Israel going out to war, the priests who are carrying the Ark are walking in front of the troops and remembering that the only living and true God is with them. The almighty God, the eternal God. The priests are remembering that He brought them through the Red Sea on dry ground, and fed them bread in the wilderness for forty years. They are reflecting on the miracle of Moses striking the rock, and water came forth to quench their thirst for forty years. Yes, the Ark of God was reminding them that God said He is one.

35

This faith must be communicated to the congregation following them. The land into which they were going was filled with peoples that serve many idols gods. Those Idols were made by man with eyes that can not see, ears that can not hear, and feet that can not walk.

God instructed the prophet Jeremiah to proclaim the message in this manner: every man is brutish by his knowledge, founders are confounded by the graven image: for his molten image is falsehood and there is no breath in them. They are vanity, the work of errors. In the time of their visitation, they shall perish (Jeremiah 51:17-18). The priests had to walk with the symbol of faith to receive their miracles. However, faith needed to be in their hearts. If they had fear, the people would have fear. If they had courage, the people would have courage. So the priests moved forward at the command of their courageous leader, Joshua. The two tables of stone with the Ten Commandments written on them must remain in the symbol of faith, the Ark of the Covenant, as a reminder that the true and living God of miracles is with them.

As the Israelites carried the law in the Ark as a symbol of remembrance, we must also carry the law or the word of God with us. Although we carry the written word with us in the Bible, we must more importantly carry the word in our hearts as a reminder. King David in Psalm 119:105-11 says, "Thy word is a lamp unto my feet and a light unto my path. Thy word have I hid in mine heart that I might not sin against thee." As long as we remember the word, we will have the victory. We will have miracles. Israel carried the word in the Ark; we must carry the word in our hearts. Mark recorded the words of Jesus in chapter 11: 22-26;

> *"Have faith in God. For verily I say unto you, that whosoever shall say unto this mountain; be thou removed and be thou cast into the sea and shall not doubt in his heart, but shall believe that those things which he says shall come to pass, he shall have whatsoever he says. Therefore, I say unto you, what things whatsoever ye desire, when ye pray, believe that ye receive them and ye shall have them. And when ye stand praying, forgive; if ye ought against any that your father, also which is in heaven may forgive you your trespasses. But if ye do not forgive, neither will your father who is in heaven forgive you your trespasses."*

Children of God, here we have a very interesting perspective of how God works.

Formula for Victory

After crossing the Jordan River on dry ground, the first obstacle that the Israelites faced in their bid to take the Promised Land was the city of Jericho. God instructed Joshua to have the men of war march around the city once per day for six days. The priests had to go before them with the Ark, the symbol of faith for their miracles, and other priests had to blow the trumpets. On the seventh day, this formula must be repeated with the added command that the people now must give a great shout at the blowing of the trumpet and the great walls of Jericho would fall flat. The Israelites followed the instructions of God through Joshua, and the events took place just as God had said. They were able to defeat the enemy (Joshua chapter 6).

Three things are important to remember that the Israelites did to ensure this miracle. First, they had the symbol of faith, the Ark, with them. Second, the word, which was found in the Ark reminded them that Jehovah is the living and true God. Third, they had confidence in the man that God had chosen to lead them. Therefore, the people of Jericho that worshiped idol gods could not defeat them. Should we not follow this formula for victory? Yes, we should.

Formula for Defeat

Converse to the victory of Jericho for the Israelites was the defeat at the hands of the people of Ai. Ai was militarily weaker than Jericho. Seemingly, the victory at Jericho would have been so easy; the leaders told Joshua that they would not need their full strength against Ai. Joshua heeded their counsel and sent a contingent of soldiers that he thought would easily defeat Ai. However, the weaker people of Ai easily killed some and chased other Israelite soldiers away. Hearing this sad news of Israel's defeat, Joshua quickly lay on his face before God. God told Joshua to get up. And that the reason Israel was defeated, was because there was sin in the camp. Beloved, when we are experiencing defeat, let us check ourselves to see if there is sin in the camp. Israel was not to have taken any of the spoils of Jericho because they were the first fruits unto God. The first fruits always belong to God. Instead, one of the soldiers, Achan, had stolen the silver and gold that belonged in the house of God. Israel had to cleanse the land by repenting. The result was the death of Achan (Joshua chapter 7).

Three things to remember in this formula that caused Israel's defeat: One, they did not carry the Ark, the symbol of faith for miracles with them. Two, they

went in pride thinking that they did not need a full
compliment of soldiers. Three, sin was in the camp.
Should we avoid this formula for defeat? Yes, we must!

The Pot Of Manna

Manna was very important to Israelites, for the
manna was a miracle in itself. God instructed Moses to
put a pot of manna in the Ark for the Israelites to
remember. That was a symbol of faith for miracles.
What did God want them to remember? God wanted
the Israelites to remember that He fed them for forty
years with a substance that had all the nutrients and
minerals to keep them healthy and without sickness for
many years. Because they were constantly on the move,
the Israelites could not plant crops with the hopes of
reaping the same. The fact that the food they brought
with them was consumed. The congregation became
very concerned about their well-being. At this point,
their faith began to wane. They seemed to have
forgotten the promise of God that He was bringing
them into a land flowing with milk and honey.

Exodus chapter 16 details the account of unbelief:

> *And they, the Israelites, took their journey*
> *from Elim and all the congregation of the children of*
> *Israel came unto the wilderness of sin, which is between*
> *Elim and Sinai, on the fifteenth day of the second month*

after their departing out of the land of Egypt. And the whole congregation of the children of Israel murmured against Moses and Aaron in the wilderness. And the children of Israel said unto them, would to God we had died by the hand of the Lord in the land of Egypt, when we sat by the fleshpots and when we did eat bread to the full. For ye have brought us forth into this wilderness to kill this whole assembly with hunger. Then said the Lord unto Moses, behold I will rain bread from heaven for you…

During my many years in the ministry, I have observed that when the people of God loose faith, one of the first manifestations of the lack thereof, is to ridicule the pastor or the church as a whole. This lack of faith usually finds an expression in the phrase, "There is no love here." The Israelites certainly did not portray an attitude of faith in God's love and care for them. It is evident that God would have fed the people. But where there is a lack of faith the result is behavior contrary to righteousness. They seem to have forgotten that it was Moses, which led them through the great miracles in Egypt and the Red Sea. So they accused him of bringing the congregation into the wilderness to kill them with hunger. However, God's divine purpose dictated that mercy be brought into the equation. He rained down bread from heaven. Nevertheless, that bread was a type of Jesus who was the true bread. Jesus taught the people concerning the true bread recorded in John chapter six verses 32:35:

> *Verily, verily I say unto you, Moses gave you not that bread from heaven; but my father gives you the true bread from heaven. For the bread of God is He which cometh down from heaven and gives life unto the world. I am the bread of life; he that cometh to me shall never hunger. And he that believeth on me shall never thirst.*

Clearly then, the manna in the wilderness was a symbol of faith for one of the greatest miracles of all time, the Lord Jesus Christ who said, "Except you eat the flesh of the son of man and drink his blood ye have no life in you. This is that bread that came down from heaven: not as your fathers did eat manna and are dead; he that eats of this bread shall live for ever" (John 6:53-58). Thanks be to God for His unspeakable gift of the bread of life. So then, when we eat the word, which is Jesus, we are eating the bread of life and it produces in us eternal life. Hallelujah!

The Communion

God commanded Moses to put a pot of manna in the Ark for the Israelites to remember how He miraculously fed them in the wilderness. It was more important for them to look down the line of time when the true bread from heaven, Jesus Christ, would be revealed to give us eternal life. The manna also typifies the communion. At the last Passover celebration that Jesus ate with His disciples, He took the unleavened bread, gave thanks to God, and broke it. He said to the disciples, "Take eat, this is my body" (Matthew 26:26). The manna in the wilderness was a symbol of faith for the powerful miracle of the bread of life. We should gladly let the powerful miracle of eternal life manifest in us.

Aaron's Rod that Budded

God instructed Moses to place Aaron's rod that budded in the Ark of the Covenant for two reasons: First, is that the Israelites might remember that when God ordained a person for ministry, God's people must not rebel against the individual that God ordained. Secondly, the budded rod would cause the Israelites to remember that God would establish His chosen leader by a miracle. Let us now consider the purpose for and the reason why the rod budded. God chose Moses and Aaron to be His leaders. Moses led the children of Israel from the bondage and slavery of Egypt to the land promised to Abraham and his seed, a land flowing

43

with milk and honey as God described it. God chose Aaron to be His first high priest. Numbers chapter 16-17 described a very pitiful and critical development in leadership rebellion among God's people. This leadership rebellion still exists today in the church. Moses wrote and left it on record in Numbers chapter 16 verses 1-4 read on to see what exactly happened:

> *Now Korah, the son of Izhar, the son of Kohath, the son of Levi, Dathan and Abiram. the sons of Eliab, and On the son of Peleth, sons of Reuben, took men: And they rose up before Moses, with certain of the children of the Israel, two hundred and fifty princes of the assembly, famous in the congregation, men of renown: And they gathered themselves together against Moses and against Aaron and said unto them, you take too much upon you seeing all the congregation is holy; everyone of them and the Lord is among them. Wherefore then lift you up yourselves above the congregation of the Lord? And when Moses heard it he fell upon his face.*

Beloved, God does not tolerate rebellion, especially leadership rebellion among His people. God responded to their rebellion by sending a plague among the people resulting in the death of 14,700 people in the congregation. Notice that only 250 leaders rebelled, but they were able to persuade 14,450 members of the congregation to engage in their rebellion. God knew every one of them that followed the rebellion and slew every one of them.

All the Leaders Rods

God further instructed Moses; to have each leader of the twelve tribes of Israel to meet Him and bring a rod. Each leader's name should be written upon the rods. God said to Moses:

> *And thou shall write Aaron's name upon the rod of Levi, for one rod shall be for the head of the house of their fathers. And thou shall lay them up in the tabernacle of the congregation before the testimony (the Ark) where I will meet with you. And it shall come to pass that the man's rod that I shall choose shall blossom: And Moses laid up the (12) rods before the Lord in the tabernacle of witness. And it came to pass that on the morrow (the next morning) Moses went into the tabernacle of witness: and, behold the rod of Aaron for the house of Levi was budded, and brought forth buds and bloomed blossoms and yielded almonds.*

Here we have a situation in Israel where the leaders were not satisfied with the position and ministry that God gave to them. So what did they do? They banded together, drew some of the congregation to

45

themselves, and brazenly said to Moses and Aaron "You take too much upon yourselves." Moses and Aaron did not *take* the authority of leading the people, God *gave* them the authority. Those leaders wanted to be where Moses and Aaron were.

Remember Lucifer? Isaiah chapter 14 reveals how Lucifer plotted against God and tried to exalt himself above his designated status, which was given to him by God. Lucifer said, "I will ascend, I will exalt, I will sit, and I will be like the most High." But God said of him, "Thou art fallen from heaven, thou art cut down to the ground." The spirit of Lucifer was in the leaders of Israel to exalt themselves against Moses and Aaron. A leader that is not satisfied with the position given to them by God, but strives unlawfully to replace chosen leaders are doing nothing but manifesting the spirit of Lucifer. God may not render swift judgment in every instance as He did to Korah and his friends, but for the unrepentant, judgment is inevitable. God sanctioned and confirmed Aaron as His chosen leader by a great sign and wonder. He chose Aaron's rod above all the rods of the other leaders to confirm in their minds that Aaron was His high priest. If God wanted to speak to the congregation, He would speak to them through Moses and Aaron. The other leaders

must take direction from Moses and Aaron. All their
rods were dry. They were staffs that they carried with
them. One of the functions of the staff was that it was
used as a sign of authority. Therefore, God said to the
other leaders, that He would do a miracle with Aaron's
rod that would leave no doubt in anyone's mind
through whom He was speaking. Overnight that dry
rod took life from the presence of God and budded
without water or earth. The dry rod blossomed and
produced almonds that could be eaten. Our great and
mighty God is still a creator. He can create for us that
which is impossible to man.

My friend, whatever your impossible situation
is, rely and trust in the living and true God. Our Lord
Jesus Christ can and will work miracles for you. Just
look for His symbols of faith that He has given you and
follow the leading of the Spirit of God.

The Symbol and the Miracle

Let me give you another personal testimony of
God's confirmation of His leaders. I was sent to a city
to minister to four people. The pastor had started the
work but decided to relocate to his hometown. I was
asked to continue the work. I had to travel almost 300
miles to do this ministry. Doing this ministry was not
easy. However, God confirmed the ministry and my

leadership to that small congregation by a mighty miracle.

The symbol of faith for that miracle was a person, and she became the symbol for her own miracle. So then, a symbol can be a person. She became the symbol by being obedient to my instruction. While speaking to her on the phone, the sister told me that she had a grave illness. This illness caused her to be very fearful of driving because she could become unconscious at any given moment. She had suffered for many years from this illness. Normally when someone tells me of a problem that he or she has, I would pray for that individual over the phone. This time the spirit of the Lord said to me, "Tell the sister that you will pray for her when you come to church on Wednesday." She obeyed my instruction and was in church at the designated time. I prayed for her in the name of Jesus Christ and she was instantly miraculously healed! Just in case you are wondering, this miracle happened in the year 2005 and she is still healed.

I am sure you will agree with the all-wise God that the rod of Aaron that budded, blossomed and yielded almonds were a fitting artifact to be placed in the Ark for a miraculous symbol of remembrance. The remembrance is not only for the Israelites, but also for us to learn from their experiences. The importance of the Ten Commandments, the Pot of Manna, and Aaron's rod that budded being placed in the Ark as a symbol of remembrance, for miracles cannot be minimized. The New Testament writer of the book of Hebrews embraced its value by including the symbols in his writings:

> *And after the second veil, the tabernacle which is called the holiest of all; which had the golden censer and the Ark of the covenant overlaid round about with gold, wherein was the golden pot that had manna, Aaron's rod that budded and the tables of the covenant. Hebrews 9:3-4.*

The Israelites carried the Ark of the Covenant around with them. They saw with their natural eyes the law of the Lord, the remembrance of God's faithfulness to sustain them with bread that had all the nutrients and vitamins to keep them healthy. And the proof of God's authority vested in the leader that He chose by displaying the dry almond rod that bore almonds overnight.

The Importance of the Almond as a Symbol of Faith for Miracles

Almonds contain vitamins, magnesium and zinc, and almonds are also a great source of protein and fiber. Eating a few almonds normally will make one feel full. Almonds, when consumed, benefit the individual by aiding in the prevention of heart disease and stress. There are two types of almond trees; one is bitter and the other sweet. One can readily see why God uses the almond tree as a symbol of faith for miracles. The sweet tree represents the blessings of God, as in Jacob's experience. The bitter tree represents the judgments of God as in the experience of Korah and his friends.[28] Jacob used the almond tree rods to create a multiplication of cattle for his benefit.

1. **Genesis 30:37 (Whole Chapter)**

   But Jacob took fresh rods of poplar and almond and plane trees and peeled white streaks in them, exposing the white in the rods.

Jacob later used almonds to present as gift to Joseph in Egypt.

2. **Genesis 43:11 (Whole Chapter)**

   And their father Israel said to them, If it must be so, now do this; take of the choicest products in the land in your sacks and carry down a present to the man, a little balm (balsam) and a little honey, aromatic spices and gum (of rock rose) or ladanum, pistachio nuts, and almonds.

God used the symbols of the lamp stands in the tabernacle.

3. Exodus 25:33 (Whole Chapter)

> *Three cups made like **almond** blossoms, each with a knob and a flower on one branch, and three cups made like **almond** blossoms on the other branch with a knob and a flower; so for the six branches coming out of the lamp stand;*

4. Exodus 25:34 (Whole Chapter)

> *And on the [center shaft] itself you shall [make] four cups like **almond** blossoms with their knobs and their flowers.*

5. Exodus 37:19 (Whole Chapter)

> *Three cups made like **almond** blossoms in one branch, each with a [calyx] knob and a flower, and three cups made like **almond** blossoms in the [opposite] branch, each with a [calyx] knob and a flower; and so*

for the six branches going out of the lamp
stand.

6. **Exodus 37:20 (Whole Chapter)**

   On [the shaft of] the lamp stand were
   *four cups made like **almond** blossoms, with*
   knobs and flowers [one at the top].

7. **Numbers 17:8 (Whole Chapter)**

   And the next day Moses went into the Tent of
   the Testimony, and behold, the rod of Aaron for the
   house of Levi had sprouted and brought forth buds and
   produced blossoms and yielded [ripe] almonds.

8. **Ecclesiastes 12:5 (Whole Chapter)**

   Also when [the old] are afraid of danger from
   that which is high, and fears are in the way, and the
   ***almond** tree [their white hair] blooms, and the*
   grasshopper [a little thing] is a burden, and desire and
   appetite fail, because man goes to his everlasting home
   and the mourners go about the streets or market-places.
   [Job 17:13]

The Lord used the almond to ensure that the
Prophet Jeremiah had the proper vision and

cognitive skills to take accurately God's message to the nations.

9. Jeremiah 1:11 (Whole Chapter)

Moreover, the word of the Lord came to me, saying, Jeremiah, what do you see? And I said I see a branch or shoot of an almond tree [the emblem of alertness and activity, blossoming in late winter.

We are to carry the word of God in our hearts. In doing so, we are constantly reminded that Jesus is the bread of life. Carrying the word of God in our hearts reminds us that the blessed man delights himself and meditates on the law of the Lord. In doing so, just as Aaron's rod budded, "He shall be like a tree planted by the rivers of water, that brings forth fruit in his season. His leaf also shall not wither and whatsoever he doeth shall prosper" (Psalm 1:1-4). Is the miracle of bearing fruit that produces prosperity working for you? If it isn't, you must become your own symbol of faith for miracles. Let the word be written in your mind and in your heart. Let the word be your meditation. Stay in the presence of God. Remember that Moses placed the rods in the presence of God. The rod that had the authority budded. The word in your heart gives you authority. We have to have Jesus abiding in and through us. As the branch cannot bear fruit of itself, except it abide in the vine, no more can ye, except ye abide in me. He that abides in Jesus will bring forth much fruit. If we do this, then we will receive what we are asking (John 15:1-7).

CHAPTER FIVE

"Faith is the substance of things hoped for, the evidence of things not seen."
Hebrews 11:1

Symbol of the Ravens

The scenario to the symbol of the cloud is recorded in 1st Kings Chapters 17-18. In chapter 17 Elijah, the prophet of the Lord, prophesied that no rain would fall for approximately three and a half years. The Lord miraculously sustained the prophet by hiding him by the brook Cherith and ordered ravens to feed him with bread and meat. The brook and the ravens became symbols of faith. The chapter continues to include the widow and her son that had only a little meal and a little oil as their total possessions. This symbol will be discussed in detail in chapter 6.

Keep in mind that the prophecy of Elijah is being fulfilled and no rain has fallen which resulted in a severe famine. After the allotted time for the fulfillment of the prophet Elijah's prophecy that there would be no rain, God speaks to him in chapter 18:1. "And it came to pass after many days that the word of the Lord came to Elijah in the third year saying, go show yourself unto (king) Ahab and I will send rain upon the earth." Keep in mind that the reason why God withheld the rain is because King Ahab and the Israelites were in the state of worshiping idols and they refused to heed the call of the prophets to return to God. But God in His abundant mercy said that He is ready to send rain upon the land. It was not without a price, however, for God was about to show His power against the false prophets of King Ahab and Queen Jezebel who prophesied for the idol god Baal.

Elijah commands King Ahab to gather 850 false prophets upon Mount Carmel, so that they could establish once and for all times who is God. Elijah summoned the Israelites also and challenged them in verse 21, "If the Lord be God follow Him, but if Baal be god then follow him."

Then Elijah establishes the criteria for proving who the true God is. First, two bulls must be chosen. One bull is for the prophets of Baal and one bull for the prophet of the Lord. The bulls were to be offered as a sacrifice. The altar was prepared and the sacrifice offered. Prayer was to be made unto God and the God that answered by fire is the true God. The prophets of the false god Baal pray from morning until the evening. They even cut themselves and became a bloody people in hopes that Baal would hear and answer them. I am reminded of the scripture in 1st

Corinthian 13 that says, "Though I give my body to be burned and have not love (for God) I am not profited." One does not have to emaciate himself to attract Gods attention. It takes faith to get God's attention. It takes faith to receive the miracle. Of course, Baal did not hear because he is not a god.

We waste our time when we take the route that leads away from God. We delay our miracle. Let us take the lesson that the prophet Elijah teaches. Now it's Elijah's turn to offer the sacrifice, he made sure the people would understand that when the fire consumes the sacrifice there was no trickery. Elijah instructs the people to pour water on the sacrifice on the altar. 1st Kings Chapter 18 verses 36-39 reads thus:

>*At the time of the offering evening sacrifice Elijah the prophet came near and said, O Lord, the God of Abraham, Isaac and Israel, let it be known this day that you are the God in Israel. And that I am your servant and that I have done all these things according your word. Hear me O Lord hear me that this people may know that you, the Lord are God and have turned their hearts back to you. Then the fire fell and consumed the burnt sacrifice, the wood, the stones, and the dust and also licked up the water that was in the trench. When the people saw it they said, the Lord He*

is God. The Lord He is God. Elijah then commands
all the four hundred and fifty false prophets to be slain.

The altar was consumed with water until the
water ran over and filled the trench that was around the
altar. The water became the symbol of faith for the
prophet Elijah. Wood, stone and dust is very difficult
to catch on fire when it is wet; moreover, when it is
very wet it becomes even more difficult. So then, the
water becomes Elijah's *symbol of faith.*

Symbol of a Man's Hand as a Cloud.

Remember that in chapter 18:1 God told the
prophet that He is ready to send rain to water the earth.
We can learn another lesson here of the workings of
God in symbols of faith to produce miracles. God is
ready to bless, but the people are not ready for God's
blessings. They had to come to the realization that it is
the living God that is sending the rain and not Baal.
Therefore, Baal had to be discredited before there eyes.
This is how God works. He is consistent. He worked
the same way among the Egyptians. God exalted
Himself against the false gods of the Egyptians before
He accomplished His great deliverance for His people
the Israelites.
Once the Israelites have come to have faith in Jehovah
alone, they are now ready and able to receive His

blessings and give to Him glory. The prophet said to
King Ahab, "...eat and drink for there is a sound of
abundance of rain" (1st Kings 18:41). Keep in mind
that rain had not fallen for over three years. The
ground was parched, and there was not a cloud in sight.
But the prophet is speaking for God. When we speak
for God, the word is sure. This is another lesson for us
to learn that we may experience continually the mighty
works of God.

Although God had spoken to Elijah that He
was ready to send rain, Elijah did not take the word for
granted. Although Elijah told Ahab that he heard the
"sound of abundance of rain," he did not go to do
other things. Elijah knew he had to see it through to
the first drop of rain. Elijah was very knowledgeable to
the fact that most miracles are accomplished when we
cooperate with God. So what did Elijah do? He went
into his prayer closet. His prayer closet was on the top
of the mountain. The picture is much brighter when
we read it. 1st Kings Chapter 18:42-46:

> So King Ahab went up to eat and drink.
> And Elijah went up to the top of (Mount) Carmel: and
> he cast himself down upon the earth and put his face
> between his knees. And said to his servant, go up now
> and look toward the sea. And he went up and looked

*and said there is nothing. And he (Elijah) said go again
seven times. And it came to pass at the seventh time
that he said, behold there ariseth a little cloud out of the
sea like a man's hand. And he said go up, say unto
King Ahab, prepare thy chariot and get thee down that
the rain stop thee not. And it came to pass at the mean
while that heaven was black with clouds and wind.
And there was a great rain. And King Ahab rode and
went to Jezreel. And the hand of the Lord was on
Elijah and he girded up his loins and ran before King
Ahab to the entrance of Jezreel.*

What a great symbol of faith is the cloud which
was the size of a man's hand. Many times, we miss a
sign because it looks very insignificant, so we discard
the symbol by saying, "Oh, that's nothing." No matter
how inconsequential the sign of the symbol may
appear, one must have faith in the God who is giving
the sign with great and mighty powers. The symbol that
is given by God is more powerful than any obstacle that
may be around. Who had faith in this scenario?
Elijah! While King Ahab went to eat, the prophet
Elijah went to pray. A cloud the size of a man's hand
seems immaterial to an abundance of rain. But the faith
of the man of God drew out of that cloud an
abundance of rain. However, the rain did not fall until

the people's faith was tested. The rain did not fall until the Israelites acknowledged that there is no other God but the Lord Jehovah. In all thy ways acknowledge Him and He shall direct thy paths (Proverbs 3:6).

CHAPTER SIX

"Faith is the substance of things hoped for, the evidence of things not seen."
Hebrews 11:1

The Widow's Little Cake

There are three basic ways that God works miracles. One, through the prayers and fasting of his people; two, through symbols of faith and three, by God's divine favor; that is, the miracle that is worked by God outside of our involvement or cooperation. For example, when the Israelites went into the land promised to them by God, they had houses to live in and food to eat that they did not build or plant. God had preordained that the land should be fruitful at the proper time for the Israelite's enjoyment. God gave the Canaanites special skills for which to build houses that would match the familial needs of the Israelites.

All miracles are worked through the instruments of faith. "But without faith it is impossible to please God."[29] God can and does work in all three ways simultaneously, or uses any combination at any given time. We must always have our spiritual eyes open to God's working. The Lord told the Apostle John to tell his people in Revelation 3:18, "Anoint thine eyes with eyesalve that thou mayest see." It is hard to see a little meal and a little oil multiplying if you do not have spiritual eyes of faith. In 1st Kings 17:9, God spoke to Elijah, to go to Zarephath and there will be a widow woman there to sustain thee. Elijah met the widow woman when she was gathering some wood to bake her last meal for her and her son. The widow woman and her son had given up hope. They believed that after they had eaten the last meal she and her son would lie down and wait for death. Elijah talked to the woman, to please, bring him some water. As she complied and got the water, Elijah told her to bring him a piece of bread also. The widow woman told Elijah, the water I can give you, but the bread I can't. All she had was a handful of meal and a little oil, and the wood that she gathered to bake the last meal for her son and her and then they would die. Elijah instructed her to go and do what he said, but bake him a cake first and bring it to him and then go and bake for you and your son. "For thus says the Lord the God of Israel, the jar of meal shall not waste away or the bottle of oil fail until the day that the Lord sends rain on the earth" (1Kings 17:14 Amplified).

Dear Reader, please examine this scenario very closely. The little meal and the little oil became her symbol of faith for her miracle from the Almighty God.

Notice that the prophet Elijah told her to bake and bring him a cake first and then bake for herself and her son to eat. The widow woman believed and obeyed the word of the prophet and went to bake Elijah the first cake. She baked him the first cake and then baked for her and her son to eat. Can you visualize the astonishment and amazement of the woman when she took of the last meal to bake the cake for Elijah and discovered that there was more meal in the barrel? When she poured the last oil, she discovered that there was more oil. Can you experience with this widow woman the joy of knowing that the Lord God had a true prophet in Israel that spoke the word of the Lord and that word was confirmed with signs following? The little meal and the little oil became her symbols of faith. The miracle produced was the meal, and the oil that increased daily. This increase was so great that she had enough to feed her household and Elijah throughout the famine. This symbol of faith and the miracle of God manifested by the widow and Elijah were so profound that Jesus referred to it in His teaching as an example of faith (Luke 4:25-26). The question now becomes, "What is in your hand? What is in your hand that God can use?"

The widow woman is a prime example of this symbol of faith. Elijah had prophesied drought and famine for three years. When things got scarce, God sent Elijah to Zarephat. God said, "I have commanded a widow woman to sustain thee."[30] It is very interesting to note that the Lord Jesus Christ used this symbol example in his teaching.[31] A tiny symbol with faith can do great miracles. Just as remarkable, if we have faith as a grain of mustard seed, we will be able to remove mountains of doubt, despair, and disappointments. This widow woman was down to her very last. A handful of meal and a little oil in a cruse. Remember that God said, "I have commanded the widow woman." The Lord Jesus did not reference the Rod of Moses in his teaching, nor did He not reference the Ark of the Covenant although, both were strong and mighty symbols of faith. Both in their use produced great feats of signs and wonders and miracles. The Lord Jesus referenced a poor widow woman, who did not even live in one of the cities of Israel. She lived in a gentile city; Sidon: Zarephat. Therefore, we can well draw the conclusion that she was a gentile. The Lord Jesus said, "But I tell you of a truth, many widows were in Israel in the days of Elijah, when the heavens were shut up three years and six months. When great famine was throughout all the land; but unto none of them was Elijah sent, save unto Sarepata (Zarephat) a city of Sidon, unto a woman that was a widow."

Why did the Lord use this symbol in his teaching? I believe the Lord used this scenario to teach us several lessons. I will explain one; I believe Jesus was showing the people that you might be in the church, but not have the faith; where faith is, He is right there. The widow woman had just enough food for one meal for her and her son. She did not have enough for a guest, but this guest was no ordinary guest. He was the man of God.

Do you have enough faith in the man of God to obey when the situation seems impossible? Do you have enough confidence in the man of God when God wants to use what you have as a symbol of faith? This is what the woman did. Her symbol of faith was a handful of meal and a little oil in a jar. For three and a half years, a handful of meal and a little oil in a jar fed the widow, her son, and the prophet Elijah. What a symbol of faith! The question is: does God work in the same manner today? Yes, He does. Remember that Jesus could do not great work in Capernaum because of the people's unbelief. Ministers, pastors, and prophets rise up in faith to believe God. Let us get a word from the Lord. Remember that God told Elijah, "I have commanded the widow woman to sustain you." Her substance was not from wealth, but from a handful of meal and a little oil in a jar. God used someone who was quick to obey. God used someone who was ready to believe. The first cake became a symbol of faith. The widow woman gave what she did not have in order to receive what she needed. There are times we have to do the same. Give something we don't have.

The prophet Elijah spoke, "For thus saith the Lord God of Israel;. The barrel of meal shall not waste; neither shall the cruse of oil fail, until the day that the Lord sendeth rain upon the earth and she went and did according to the saying of Elijah: and she and he, and her house, did eat many days."[32] Let us look at the phrase, "and her house," (I Kings 17:15). At the beginning of the conversation, it's, "me and my son" (I Kings 17:12). Then Elijah was introduced, and the words became me and my son and Elijah. The work of God is being fulfilled; the meal and the oil increased. Then the words became me, my son, and Elijah and my house. What a miracle from a little cake!

Many people are in need of God great miracles today. We need prophets of God that can say, "thus says the Lord," for those miracles to be performed.

Too many deceivers are saying "thus says the Lord," and the Lord has not sent them. That is why many do not have their miracle. Let me give you wise counsel. Pray that the Lord will send you, an Elijah that can say "thus says the Lord" and the words are fulfilled.

The Mantle and the Rod

Elijah's mantle was used three times as a symbol of faith. The first recorded time that Elijah used his mantle was when God told him to anoint Elisha to be prophet in his stead (1Kings 19:16-21). Elijah cast his mantle upon Elisha as a symbol that God was calling him into service. The second time that Elijah used his mantle was when the Lord told Elijah that he would be taken up from the earth. Elijah started his journey from Gilgal. Elisha was being groomed to step into the office of the lead prophet. 2 Kings 2 gives us the story. Elijah told Elisha to stay there because the Lord has sent him to Bethel. (The meaning of Bethel is house of God). The Lord had revealed to Elisha what he was doing. Let us learn from the attitude and spirit of Elisha. He is contemplating the awesome responsibility he is about to receive. His reply? "As the Lord liveth and as thy soul liveth I will not leave thee." So they went to Bethel. There were 50 sons of the prophets at Bethel.

Again, Elijah told Elisha to go there because He is sending him to Jericho. The Lord also revealed to the sons of the prophets that Elijah would be taken up to heaven that day.

Elisha knew this however, he instructed the sons of the prophets to hold their peace. So many times young men glory in a revelation that God shows to them. Elisha's attitude and spirit says this is not the time to glory in revelation. Hold your peace.

Here was a great opportunity to rule. Elisha didn't have to build a congregation; there were already 50 saved individuals to start. Here was a great opportunity for Elisha to build a congregation, but he did not.

Elisha's response was: Hold your peace. God has a greater plan for the situation. The scenario was repeated at Jericho. Again, Elisha's response is the same. We need more people with the Elisha spirit. The spirit of Elisha is the spirit to be a follower, the spirit to be a servant, the spirit of loyalty and willingness to minister to your leader. The scripture says of Elisha; "He arose and went after Elijah, and ministered unto him."[33]

Conversely, there is an Absalom spirit. What is the Absalom spirit? Absalom sat in the King's gate and turned the heart of the people away from his father King David to himself. However, Absalom died like a fool (II Samuel 18:9-18).

Elisha continued to follow Elijah. The last leg of the journey was the crossing of the river Jordan. Elijah told Elisha to stay, because the Lord sent him. Elisha already had a congregation of 50. Again, Elisha said, "No, I am going with you," so they went to Jordan. Of course the water was in their way (II Kings 2:8), and Elijah took his mantle (a faith symbol) wrapped it together, and smote the waters. The water divided so that they went over on dry ground. This was the second recorded time that Elijah used his mantle. The mantle became a symbol of faith for both Elijah and Elisha. God honored the faith of Elijah. The anointing was flowing. Faith was at a high level.

"....Elijah said unto Elisha, "Ask what I shall do for thee..." (II Kings 2:9). Did Elisha say, "Make me ruler over the fifty sons of the prophets at Bethel and fifty sons of the prophets of Jericho?" No! Many run after the numbers to command without the spirit of God. We cannot rule effectively over God's people without His spirit. We cannot effectively use the symbol of faith without the faith in God.

Elisha told Elijah, that he wanted a double portion of the Holy Ghost that he had. He also wanted a double portion of the holy anointing. Many of us believed that no one in the Old Testament era possessed the Holy Ghost and that the spirit of God only came upon them to empower the men and women of God, rather than for a work to be completed. When a work is done, that empowerment was then lifted. However, I believe that the Holy Ghost was not available or given to everyone. I also believe that the Spirit of God came upon certain men, as in the case of Samson, for a specific work. But, I also believe that men like Abraham and all of God's prophets that spoke in the name of the Lord possessed the Holy Ghost. I Peter 1:10-11, the Apostle Peter states ..."the spirit of Christ which was in them..." I believe Elijah was full of the Holy Ghost. Up until this time, Elisha did not yet have the Holy Ghost. That is why he did not stop at Gilgal. That is why Elisha went to Jordan. Elisha was being tutored to fulfill the prophet's office. He knew he needed the anointing. Elisha responded, "Elisha, you have asked a hard thing; but if you see me when I go, you shall have what you asked for." Elijah has now become a symbol of faith to Elisha. Elijah answered, "If you see me when I go." We have to see something.

71

When God uses anything or anyone as a symbol of faith, we must see beyond that symbol; for beyond the symbol is a sign, a wonder, a miracle, an anointing. If we only see the symbol, we will pass it off as nothing. Faith is the substance of things hoped for, the evidence of things not seen (Hebrews 11:1).

Elisha now has to keep his eyes on Elijah. The sign, the wonder, the miracle, and the anointing will come only, "if you see me." Elijah was caught up. Elisha saw him. Elijah's mantle fells to the ground. Elisha picked it up. The mantle became the next symbol of faith for Elisha.

In the beginning of our faith walk, the Lord God often starts us out with symbols of faith until our faith grows to a grain of mustard seed. Then we can say to the mountain, "Be thou removed." God meets us at our level of faith, in order to take us to His level of faith. Elijah is caught up to heaven, full of the Holy Ghost. God honored Elisha's request and gave him a double portion of the anointing he had given Elijah. Now he is ready. Now he steps into the office of the prophet. He must re-cross Jordan, 2 Kings 2:11-15:

> *And it came to pass as they still went on, and talked, that behold there appeared a chariot of fire, and horses of fire and parted them both asunder; and Elijah went up by*

a whirlwind into heaven and Elisha saw it and he cried, my father, my father, the chariot of Israel and the horsemen thereof. And he saw him no more: and he took hold of his own clothes, and rent them in two pieces. He took up also the mantle of Elijah that fell from him, and went back, and stood by the bank of Jordan; And he took the mantle of Elijah that fell from him, and smote the waters, and said, Where is the LORD God of Elijah? And when he also had smitten the waters, they parted hither and thither: and Elisha went over. And when the sons of the prophets, which were to view at Jericho saw him, they said, The spirit of Elijah doth rest on Elisha. And they came to meet him, and bowed themselves to the ground before him.

Where is the God of Elijah? He was right there. The symbol of faith is the mantle that parted the waters. The Sons of the Prophets recognized that Elisha's prayers have been answered. He has the double portion of the anointing. The sons of the prophets now had a new reverence for Elisha. They bowed themselves to the ground. What a difference from the first meeting! In today's vernacular, the conversation went something like this. "Hey man, don't you know the Lord is going to take your main man today." "Yeah, I know, chill for a moment" - very casual, very light, but now with a new respect and a new honor. They bowed themselves to the ground. Isn't it better to have the Lord's honor rather than to seed your own honor? Remember all this came about by the word of the prophet. How much confidence do you have in your leader to receive a word from him? On the other hand, if you are not getting a word from your leader, through preaching, teaching, or one-on-one directive, you may need a new leader from God.

Elisha truly had a double portion of Elijah's spirit, that is, the spirit of God, which was in Elijah. The life of Elisha was filled with miracles. We all need houses in which to live. It was no different in Elisha's time. The sons of the prophets needed houses in which to live. 2nd Kings Chapter 6 gives us a graphic illustration of how to own our own homes. In relating this procedure, we can observe a very interesting miracle and the symbol that created it. The miracle is the iron that swam, and the symbol that produced the miracle is a piece of stick. Let us read verses 1-7: (Amplified)

> *And the sons of the prophets said unto Elisha,*
> *look now, the place where we live before you is too small*
> *for us. Let us go to the Jordan, and each man get there*
> *a house beam; and let us make us a place there where we*
> *may dwell. And he answered, go. One said, be pleased*
> *to go with your servants. He answered, I will go. So he*

went with them. And when they came to the Jordan,
they cut down trees. But as one was felling his beam, the
axe-head fell into the water. And he cried, my master
for it was borrowed. And the man of God said,, where
did it fall? When shown the place, Elisha cut off a stick
and threw it in there and the iron floated. He said, pick
it up. And he put out his hand and took it.

(2 Kings 6:1-7)

Do you want to own your own home? If you do
own your own home now, and are in need of a larger
home? Or if you do not own yet, the solution is to find
a true prophet and consult with him. This is what the
sons of the prophet did. Notice that they relied on the
man of God to see them through every phase. There
are three points to consider in the development of this
scenario. One, the sons of the prophets consulted with
the man of God. (verse 1) Two, they identified the
place where they wanted to live (verse 2). Three, they
wanted the man of God to see them through the whole
process of development (verse 3). Beloved, this
method is a time-tested process of receiving our
miracles. God has put in our system of communication
with Him, prophets or men of God and pastors. When
we have need of a sure word, we can consult with them.
If you are not in contact with one or more of these men

or women of God, you need to find one. How do you recognize one who is truly called and chosen of God? Note: called and chosen-for one must not only be called, one must be chosen. The chosen is one who is usually dedicated and consecrated. God usually establish that particular one by signs and wonders. What do you look for? One of the signs that you can look for and verify is: does the man or woman of God have a verifiable word of knowledge? For example, if you read further in 2nd Kings Chapter 6 you will observe that after the axe-head miracle what the prophet Elisha gave a verifiable word of knowledge. Verses 8-10 reads thus:

> Then the king of Syria warred against the King of Israel and took counsel with his servants saying, in such and such a place shall be my camp. Then the man of God (Elisha) sent unto the King of Israel saying, beware that thou pass not such a place for the Syrians are coming down there. Then the King of Israel sent to the place of which Elisha told and warned him. Thus, he protected and saved himself repeatedly.

The most reliable sign, I believe, you can look for is the sign that the man or woman of God will not compromise the integrity of the word of God. When going to the man or woman of God, you must have a plan of action. You may not have all your "ducks in a row" when you consult with the man or woman of God, but a least you should have some idea of what you want. The man or woman of God can then help you to identify certain things. Keep the man or woman of God informed throughout the whole process. You must also be aware that these men and women of God do not know everything, but they know enough to bring you your miracle.

The stick: Symbol of faith that resulted in the axe-head miracle.

If Elisha, the prophet had not been with the sons of the prophets, they would not have experienced the miracle of the swimming axe-head. While cutting down the tree to make the beam, the axe-head fell into the water. The man of God cut a stick from the tree and threw it into the water where the axe-head fell (2 King 6).

Please note two things here: the great faith of the man of God and his knowledge in knowing what to do. Elisha had to have faith in his own symbol of faith, the stick from the tree. The same tree that ejected the axe-head is the same tree that became the symbol for the miracle. The power of faith in the symbol of faith thrown in the place where the axe-head drowned caused the iron to come to the surface of the water and swim. The son of the prophet reached out and took it. What a miracle!! You, too, can have great miracles. Just follow the process.

The widow of one of the prophets

The examples that God gives us in the scriptures are so plain:

> Now there cried a certain women of the wives of the sons of the prophets unto Elisha saying, thy servant my husband is dead, and thou knowest that thy servant did fear the Lord. And the creditor is come to take unto him my two sons to be bondmen. And Elisha said unto her, what shall I do for thee? Tell me, what hast thou in thy house? And she said, thine handmaid hath not anything in the house, save a pot of oil. Then he said, go, borrow the vessels abroad of all thy neighbors, even empty vessels, borrow not a few. And when thou art come in, thou shalt shut the door upon thee and upon thy sons, and shalt pour out into all those vessels, and thou shalt set aside that which if full. So she went from him and shut the door upon her and upon her sons, who brought the vessels to her, and she poured out. And it came to pass, when the vessels were full, that she said unto her son; bring me yet a vessel. And he said unto her, there is not a vessel more. And the oil stayed.

When she came and told the man of God, he said, go sell
the oil and pay thy debt and live thou and thy children of
the rest (2 Kings 4:1-7).

Tremendous blessing would follow, if we
pursue the guidelines of the Word of God. In general,
saints don't utilize their leaders effectively.
Unfortunately, when some do, the leader is not able to
give them a word from the Lord. Here is the widow
of a prophet who had died and left her in debt. Some
preachers work very hard in the kingdom of God and
never realize financial gain. This is a classic example.
The widow told the prophet that her husband likewise
was a prophet that feared the Lord; however, he left
here in debt. Instead of feeling sorry, she went to the
man of God who had a word for her. She knew that
they would take her sons as slaves in exchange for the
debt owed. This is the first thing we need is a man of
God. If you don't have a man of God in your life, I
counsel you to find a man of God. Put yourself in
submission to him. Before it is all over, you will need a
man of God. So many times saints come to me
expecting to get some resources that I don't have.
When I give them, a word and they don't follow and
obey that word because they have it in their mind the
way I should bless them. Remember Peter and John

were going up to the temple to pray and met a man that had paralysis in the limbs. Acts Chapter 3:1-6, "Silver and gold have I none." The prophet wanted to know what she had in her house. You have what it takes to bring the blessing, if you believe. I don't have anything but a little oil. But what is that, that is nothing. Remember that God can take nothing and make something. Go and borrow vessels. Do not limit yourself. Do not limit God. The little oil now became a symbol of faith. Get all the vessels you can. A miracle is about to take place.

A personal testimony of one of the miracles that took place in one of our Miracles on Monday services is when I prophesied to a minister that was traveling to another country. I told him that when he arrived at the airport, he would meet a man who would help him with what he needs, when he arrived and got settled at his destination, he called back and testified that the word of God was fulfilled.

Jesus said go into your secret closet and pray. Your father is there with you. He will reward you openly. Many distractions may arise to keep one from realizing his or her miracle and to prevent it from taking place. Woman, shut the door. Man, shut the door. You don't need any interference. Sometimes in a service, God wants to do great things. There can be hindrances. Shut the door. You need total concentration to carry out the task. When you shut the door, begin to pour out the oil into the vessels. "Son! bring me another vessel." "Mother, there are no more vessels." The oil of the anointing is flowing. Faith is at high level, the symbol of faith is producing. When you are in that high level of anointing, you don't want to stop. Time constrains us – physically we are constrained, even when one stops, the anointing yet flows. As long as there are vessels, oil will flow from the little jar. "What's next man of God? Sell the oil, pay your debt. Live off the rest." Jesus Christ is the same yesterday, today, and forever. I am God, I change not. "Prove me now herewith," saith the Lord. Prove all things. But seek ye first the kingdom of God and His righteousness and all these things will be added unto you. Use the man of God. We have seen the strong usage of symbols of faith by God in the Old Testament to generate signs wonders and miracles. The questions should be now; does God use symbols of faith in the New Testament?

CHAPTER SEVEN

"Faith is the substance of things hoped for, the evidence of things not seen."
Hebrews 11:1

Is the symbol of faith needed in the church?

I believe God works the same way today. He does not change. I believe the Lord Jesus himself used symbols of faith in His ministry. "Faith is the substance of things hoped for, and the evidence of things not yet seen" (Hebrew 11:1), with the natural eye. Twice Jesus used the symbol of a few loaves and fish to feed thousands. Does this sound familiar? John Chapter 6 records this miracle that was produced by a symbol of faith. Five thousand men followed Jesus. Jesus asked Philip, "Whence shall we buy bread that these may eat?"[34] Philip answered Jesus, "Two hundred penny worth of bread is not sufficient for them, that every one of them may take a little."[35] What was Philip saying to Jesus? We don't have what it takes to feed so many people. We do not have the resources. Andrew said to Jesus, "There is a lad here, who has five barley loaves and two small fish, but what is that among so many?" Forty dollars is not enough to buy food that each person could have a taste, five barley loaves and two fish is not enough to feed five thousand men beside women and children. Jesus wanted "to prove" Philip - for Jesus himself knew what he would do. Jesus made the men sit down. Jesus took the loaves and the fishes, and it had to be given to Him. We must be willing to give God what He asks for in order to receive a multiplication. Jesus gave thanks and began to break the loaves and then the fish. Remember the oil and the vessels. Jesus gave thanks. We must give thanks. That which was not enough to give everybody a taste, became enough to fill more than five thousand people to the full. They ended up with more than they started. They had twelve baskets full of leftovers.

Matthew 15:29-39 records another event. Jesus went up into the mountain. They brought unto him the lame, blind, dumb, maimed and many others and Jesus healed them. For three days Jesus was ministering and healing people, then he said to the disciples:

I have compassion on the multitude, because they continue now with me three days and have nothing to eat. And I will not send them away fasting for they will faint in the way. Jesus saith unto them, how many loaves do you have? They told Jesus, seven and a few little fish; Jesus "took the seven loaves and the fish, and gave thanks, and brake them, and gave to his disciples, and the disciples gave to the multitude."

Four thousand men besides women and children were fed. What do we have that the Lord Jesus can use as a symbol of faith? Perhaps three days fasting, or prayer is that not enough to share of something? Faith says, if I give it, I will have abundance. So I willingly give it to Jesus. The return is not measurable. This is how Jesus answered Peter's question, Matthew 19:27-29:

> *Then answered Peter and said unto Jesus, behold we have forsaken all (We have given to you ourselves as symbols of faith) and followed thee. What shall we have therefore? And Jesus said unto them, verily I say unto you, that ye which have followed me in the regeneration when the Son of Man shall sit in the throne of his glory, ye also shall sit upon twelve thrones judging the twelve tribes of Israel.*

This is where we come in. "Everyone that has forsaken houses, or brethren, or sisters or father, or mother, or wife, or children, or lands, for my name's sake, shall receive an hundred fold and shall inherit everlasting life" (Matthew 19:29). How can one describe this promise? Let us prove and experience this great promise. Let us give ourselves as a symbol of faith to God for His divine purpose.

Peter's Shadow

The Apostle Peter was walking strongly in the Holy Ghost, and signs and wonders were being wrought through him physically. He could not get to all the people to minister to them in all their needs. However, faith was being magnified. The people took hold onto the faith of God. Because of the increased faith among the people, Apostle Peter's shadow became a symbol of faith. Acts 5:12, "...and by the hands of the Apostles were many signs and wonders wrought among the people and they were all with one accord in Solomon's porch." Vs. 14, "...and believers were the more added to the Lord, multitudes both of men and women." Vs. 15-16, "Insomuch that they brought forth the sick into the streets and laid them on beds and couches that at least the shadow of Peter passing by might overshadowed some of them. There came also a multitude out of the cities round about unto Jerusalem, bringing sick folks and those who were vexed with unclean spirits and they were healed everyone." Beloved, Jesus Christ is the same yesterday, today, and forever. The Holy Ghost is the same today. The Apostle Peter was not a superhuman, just a man full of the Holy Ghost. When you follow a leader that is full of the Holy Ghost and the anointing, let your faith rise.

Let your confidence be firm. Just a touch, just to be in His presence. Just the shadow overshadowing you can bring your miracle. What is the failure? We are not with one accord. We do not have the confidence and faith in God that He can do those things today and work in the same measure. Come on, saints, and children of God. Let us return to believing the scriptures as the early church did. Let us put away pride and arrogance. God is willing to work with us (or rather, we with him), for us and through us. To touch the man of God by faith, remember the woman who touched the hem of Christ's garment.

The Hem of His garment

"And a certain woman which had an issue of blood twelve years" (Mark 5:25), how long have you been suffering? A certain woman could be anybody. It could be you. She went from doctor to doctor. Some of you go from church to church, looking, seeking for help, seeking for healing, searching for deliverance. Her condition grew worse. Does this sound familiar? Vs. 27 "When she had heard of Jesus, came in the press behind, and touched his garment." Vs. 28, for she said, "If I may touch the border of his garment." The result is she was immediately made whole. You are going from doctor to doctor, from church to church, from psychiatrist to psychiatrist. But have you heard of Jesus?

Jesus who works through the symbols of faith. Jesus who has an answer to every problem. Jesus who is the same yesterday, today, and forever. The woman said within herself, "If I may touch." The symbol, the go between, the hem, the border, and the garment became her symbol of faith. The crowd is around Jesus, she blocked out the crowd from her mind, and her full focus was on the symbol of faith. If I but touch, I shall be made whole. If I give God what he asks for, if I give something of value to God, if I present my body as a living sacrifice, I shall have my miracle. I shall have my deliverance. "Who touched my clothes," Jesus asked. The disciples answered, "Master, all these people around you and you asked who touched you?" Christ shared with them that it was not about people pushing, but, someone with faith just touched him. Faith had drawn virtue from the hem; faith had drawn healing from the border. I felt it leave my body. Oh Lord our God help us that when we need that miracle, when we need to use a symbol of faith we will do the same and draw faith from Jesus. The woman said, "It's me Lord." Jesus said, Mark 5:34, "Daughter, thy faith hath made thee whole, go in peace and be whole of thy plague."

Each leader must stay full of the Holy Ghost and have faith that when the people's faith rises to the level where a touch or a shadow will move God to work in their behalf. I strongly believe the words of Jesus. "Greater works than these shall ye do, because I go to the father" "As my father hath sent me, so send I you" (John 14:12).

Item from the Body

How do we know if God will do something if we don't ask him? If we don't have faith, nothing works. Without faith, it is impossible to please God. Even if God orders it, and we don't believe it, it does not work. If a saint or Child of God has the faith to believe that the shadow of the man of God passing will heal and bring deliverance, it will work (John 15:7-9). "If ye abide in me, and my words abide in you, ye shall ask what ye will, and it shall be done unto you. Herein is my father glorified, that ye bear much fruit so shall ye be my disciples" (Acts 19: 11-12). "And God wrought special miracles by the hand of Paul, so that from his body were brought unto the sick, handkerchiefs or aprons (or towels) and the diseases departed from them, and the evil spirits went out of them." The Lord spoke to me and said distribute prayer towels. Not long after a young girl got pregnant, she developed complications that threatened both her and the baby's life. The child's mother testified that she took one of the prayer towels and massaged her daughter's stomach with prayer. The daughter gave birth to a healthy baby and both the mother and child are doing well. The people could not bring the sick to Paul, so they brought items from his body. Not only were the sick healed, but also demons were cast out of many. Faith is the substance of things hoped for, the evidence of things not seen. God honors faith and according to your faith, so be it unto you. Throughout the Bible, God uses symbols of faith to do great miracles, Jesus Christ the same yesterday, today and forever,-Amen.

CHAPTER EIGHT

Faith is the substance of things hoped for, the evidence of things not seen.

Hebrews 11:1

Crippled Faith and the Bed Symbol

The man had an infirmity for thirty-eight years. He had a story to tell. The Apostle John recorded his story:

> *Now there is at Jerusalem by the sheep market a pool, which is called in the Hebrew tongue Bethesda, having five porches. In these (porches) lay a great number of impotent folk, of blind, halt, withered, waiting for the moving of the water. For an angel went down at a certain season into the pool, and troubled the water: whosoever then first after the troubling of the water stepped in was made whole of whatsoever disease he had. And a certain man was there, which had an infirmity thirty and eight years. When Jesus saw him lie, and knew that he had been now a long time in that case, He saith unto him, wilt thou be made whole? The impotent man answered Him, sir, I have no man, when the water is troubled, to put me into the pool, but while I am coming, another stepped down before me. Jesus saith unto him, rise, take up thy bed and walk. And immediately the man was made whole and took up his bed and walked. (John 5:2-9)*

Crippled Faith.

Thirty-eight years is a long time. What was this man's thought pattern? Did he call for someone to help him? Thirty-eight years of lying in that position and waiting for someone to put him in the water had crippled his faith. Many times people give up on God when the answer is not readily available. Their faith becomes crippled. Notice again the question that Jesus asked the crippled man. "Wilt thou be made whole" (John 5:16)? The man with the crippled faith answered Jesus, "I have no man' (John 5:7). A great faith anticipation answer to that question should have been, "Yes, sir! I want to be made whole." But his faith was crippled, so he answered, "I have no man." So many times, we answer a faith challenge by saying, "I don't know how," or, "it can't be done," or, "I have no resources."

A Personal Testimony

I have a very poignant experience of crippled faith. Early in my marital life, my wife and I decided to purchase a house. We did purchase the house after many trials of our faith. Lack of money was a factor and part of this trying experience. We were very happy when it was all over and we eventually settled into our new home. Shortly after we moved into our new home,

91

an opportunity presented itself to us. We were given the choice to sell our home and purchase another house at quite a substantial price below market value. I allowed the devil to cripple my faith. He presented to me the difficulty we had in purchasing our home. We bought into his plan instead of looking at the victory that God had given to us. Our crippled faith would not allow us to move ahead. In a few years, the market value increased. You, too may have had occurrences in your life, where your faith was crippled, list some of them, and let God know, "No longer will I have crippled my faith!" Here we were left to be content to stay in the house *we* chose. Our symbol of faith was the real estate agent who said to us, "I will help you." We did not use our symbol of faith. Notwithstanding, we have learned our lesson. Thank God for His great mercies. From here on let our faith increase!

Crippled Faith Made Strong

Jesus said to the impotent man, "rise and take your bed and walk." The impotent man's bed became his symbol of faith. The only way that he could walk is to take up his bed. Jesus challenged him. He was crippled for thirty-eight years. He was dependent on someone to put him into the water as soon as the angel had troubled it. Would he be asking someone to take up his bed? Thank God he met the challenge of Jesus and saw his symbol of faith. The crippled man stooped down, took up his bed and he knew immediately that he could walk. And walk he did. His faith was no longer crippled. He no longer was waiting on someone else to do it for him. The man took up the bed himself and walked. What an amazing example of a crippled faith made strong!

The Hem of His Garment, revisited Symbol of Faith

A similar example to the impotent man's story, remember the woman with the issue of blood, in Matthew chapter 9:20-22. This woman had an issue of blood for 12 years. Mark 5:25-34 records that she had gone to many doctors, but her condition only got worse. The woman heard about Jesus and His healing power. "So then faith comes by hearing and hearing by the word of God" (Romans 10:17). The woman said within, "If I may but touch the hem of His garment I shall be whole." She had inner conviction. She made her own symbol of faith. She made the garment of Jesus her symbol of faith. Mark said there was a crowd around Jesus. The woman did not allow the crowd to stop her. She knew that she needed a miracle. She had been suffering for twelve long years and getting worse.

The doctors could not cure her. "I must touch my symbol of faith," she must have said within herself. She touched the hem of Jesus' garment and immediately she was healed from her sickness of twelve years. Jesus said to her, "Your faith has made you whole" (Mark 5:34).

Create your own Symbol of Faith

The woman with the issue of blood created her own symbol of faith. You can as well. Get a bottle of olive oil, have the man of God bless it and pray over it, and make it your symbol of faith. Use your symbol to anoint by faith objects, things, or situations that need to be changed, and allow God to do the work. Jesus Christ is the same yesterday, today, and forever. He will do it for you. Your symbol of faith could be a special gift offering. Look around you. Ask Jesus to help you. He will.

CHAPTER NINE

"Faith is the substance of things hoped for, the evidence of things not seen."
Hebrews 11:1

Symbol of Faith and the Miracles of God for Ministry

Ephesians 4:3 tells us that the gifts of Apostles, Prophets, Evangelists, Pastors, and Teachers are miracle gifts for ministry to perfect the church. They are miracle gifts because the gifts are not learned. They are given miraculously to individuals by God. I have chosen the gift of prophet to illustrate this chapter. I have also chosen the Prophet Ezekiel as my subject. In Ezekiel chapters 2-3, he had seen visions of God, four living creatures, and the four wheels and wheels in the middle of the wheels. Ezekiel had seen unfolding fires. Ezekiel had seen the mighty power of God. Nevertheless, to prophecy God showed Ezekiel a simpler symbol. Ezekiel found a roll.

The Roll

God told Ezekiel to eat what he found. He showed Ezekiel a roll, (a document) which Ezekiel had to eat in order to prophecy. The roll now became Ezekiel's symbol of faith for ministry. If Ezekiel did not eat the roll, he would not be able to speak or prophecy. The roll was a symbol of the word of God.

The prophet opened his mouth and ate the roll. What had Ezekiel eaten? He had eaten the word of God: A Symbol. Romans 10: 17 spoke to us in this manner:

> *So then faith cometh by hearing and hearing by the word of God.*

Ezekiel had been sent to speak or prophecy to the Israelites that were in captivity and those that were yet in Jerusalem. God made sure that Ezekiel understood the mission and that he must proceed by faith and not by sight. It was the word *of* God that he must speak, "Fill thy bowels with this roll" (Ezekiel 3:3). He ate the roll and it was sweet as honey in his mouth. I am reminded of the Psalmist who said, "O taste and see that the Lord is good, blessed is the man that trusts in Him" (Psalm 34:8). I personally have experienced the sweetness of the word of God in my meditation and in the ministry of the word. The Bible is the roll. Have you ate the whole roll and experienced its sweetness? If you have not eaten the whole roll, then please do it now. If you do not, you are missing the opportunity to use a symbol of faith to activate a miracle that you need.

Once Ezekiel had eaten the roll, God told him to go and speak words to the Israelites. Keep in mind that symbols and miracles are not only for our blessings, but they are for God's benefit as well. God uses symbols and miracles for His glory. The burning bush symbol, although it produced miracles on behalf of the Israelites, actually was for ministry. The ministry of Moses was to prove to Pharaoh and the Egyptians that the God of Abraham, Isaac, and Jacob is the only living and true God. He is the eternal that created the heavens and the earth. God himself said so, "I Am." The last symbol of faith for the miracle of deliverance for the Israelites from the bondage of Egypt was the symbol of blood. As the blood became a symbol of deliverance for the Israelites, it also became a symbol of judgment for the Egyptians to prove to them that their gods were not gods.

The Symbol of Blood

Exodus 12 tells the story about how that God instructed the Israelites to kill a lamb and put the blood on their doorpost, for that very night an angel would go through the land and all the houses that had no blood on their doorpost the first-born in that house would die. Exodus 12:12 gives us the reason why and the purpose for God taking that particular action:

> *For I will pass through the land of Egypt this night and will smite all the firstborn in the land of*

97

Egypt, both man and beast. And against all the gods of
Egypt I will execute judgment. I AM THE LORD.

When Pharaoh realized that, the blood had
become a symbol of judgment for the Egyptians and a
symbol of deliverance for the Israelites he hastily
executed the order for the Israelites to leave Egypt. He
was not convinced that God is the only Lord. His
mindset was to avert further judgment. There are many
people with that type of mindset today. In my ministry,
I have the opportunity to minister to some people who
only want deliverance from trouble. These individuals
do not want the blood of Jesus to wash their sins away.
They do not want the deliverance that brings salvation.
They want me to pray for them so that the unjust judge
will have mercy on them or that they will receive some
financial blessings. Just like Pharaoh, these types of
people wanted to prevent or escape something that
would affect them negatively. They do not want the
deliverance that will have an effect on them spiritually.
However, our merciful God continues to be
longsuffering to all humanity in blessing them for the
express purpose of defining His will to them. Such was
the order in Ezekiel's day and God is dealing with the
Israelites.

The Lord God almighty who has a tremendous love for humankind continues to prevail upon man to come and have fellowship with Him. God said to Ezekiel, "I am not sending you to a people that do not understand your language." However, God said the Israelites would not hear. Analogously speaking, the writers of the New Testament voice similar pronouncements from God. The Apostle Paul writing to Timothy in Chapter 2, exhorts him to, "Preach the word, and be instant in season, out of season." For the time will come when they, the people, will not endure sound doctrine; but after their own lusts shall they heap to themselves teachers having itching ears. Moreover, they shall turn away their ears from the truth and believe fables" (2 Timothy 4:2-4).

Confirmation of the Ministry

In Hebrews chapter 2, we read these words:

> *Therefore we ought to give the more earnest heed to the things which we have heard, lest at any time we should let them slip. For if the word spoken by angles was steadfast, and every transgression and disobedience received a just recompense of reward, how shall we escape if we neglect so great salvation; which at first began to be spoken by the Lord and was confirmed to them that heard Him. God also bearing them, ministers, witness,*

both with signs and wonders, symbols, and different
miracles and gifts of the Holy Ghost according to His
own will.

It becomes clear that God uses symbols of faith for miracles to establish the ministry for the express purpose of revealing Himself to humanity in order that they might come to the knowledge of salvation.

CHAPTER TEN

"Faith is the substance of things hoped for, the evidence of things not seen."
Hebrews 11:1

The Resurrection

Now faith is the assurance (the confirmation, the title deed) of the things (we) hope for, being the proof of things (we) do not see and the conviction of their reality. (Faith perceiving as real fact what is not revealed to the senses.) (Hebrews 11:1 Amplified)

Our ultimate hope is the resurrection. Our ultimate faith is to see our loving Lord Jesus Christ. The Lord Jesus made Lazarus a symbol of faith to illustrate to us the resurrection. John 11 records that Lazarus was dead for four days when Jesus went to his city of Bethany. The sisters of Lazarus, Mary, and Martha said to Jesus, "If you had been here, our brother would still be living." Jesus said to them, "I am the resurrection and the life." "He that believeth in me, though he were dead, yet shall he live, and whosoever liveth and believeth in me shall never die." Then He asked them, "Do you believe this" (John 11:21-26 John 11; 32)? Jesus interjected here that He was the symbol of faith for the resurrection and the resurrection itself. However, Jesus went to the grave of Lazarus and with a loud voice said to the dead man, "Lazarus come forth."

Lazarus who was dead for four days came out of the grave alive. We must believe the Word of God, the Bible irrefutably tells us that there will be a resurrection of the dead (Daniel 12:2, 1st Thessalonians 4: 13-18, Revelation 20:4-6).

On the resurrection rests all of humanity's hope of salvation. All that God had been doing from the beginning was pointing to the resurrection. The burning bush symbol with Moses' objective was the deliverance of Israel from the bondage of Egypt. When Israel passed through the Red Sea, it was a type of the death burial and resurrection of Jesus. The Apostle Paul writing in 1st Corinthians 10:1-2 explained this principle:

> *Moreover brethren, I would not that ye should be ignorant, how that all our fathers were under the cloud and all passed through the sea and were all baptized unto Moses in the cloud and in the sea.*

The Apostle further substantiated this revelation in his letter to the Romans.

> *Know ye not that so many of us as were baptized into Jesus Christ were baptized into His death? Therefore we are buried with Him by baptism into death: that like as Christ was raised up from the dead by the glory of the father, even so we should walk in*

newness of life. For if we have been planted together in the likeness of His death, we shall be also in the likeness of His resurrection; knowing this, that our old man is crucified with Him, that the body of sin might be destroyed, that henceforth we should not serve sin. For he that is dead is freed from sin. Now if we be dead with Christ, we believe that we shall also live with Him. Knowing that Christ being raised from the dead, dieth no more; Death hath no more dominion over Him. For in that He died, He died unto sin once; but in that He liveth He liveth unto God. Likewise, reckon ye also yourselves to be dead indeed unto sin, but alive unto God through our Lord Jesus Christ (Romans 6:3-11).

Therefore, the resurrection principle as a symbol of faith is clearly. It has its ultimate fulfillment in Jesus Christ. This principle is manifested through the love of God for us. When Adam ate of the fruit in the Garden of Eden, he found himself to be naked, for God had said he should not eat of that tree. Eating of the tree brought death to Adam. Consequently, all of Adam's children, and humankind, died along with Adam. Christ then became our symbol of faith.

As Moses was went closer to the bush that burned and not consumed, so we should come closer to Christ as God's symbol of faith. The Lord's death, burial, and resurrection likewise are the symbol of faith in order that we may receive eternal life in the world to come. As God spoke to Moses from the burning bush, so Christ speaks to us through His death, Burial, and resurrection. Jesus calls us with a special calling. The Apostle records Jesus' call. "Come unto me all ye that labor and are heaven laden and I will give you rest" (Matthew 11:28). The author of the book of Hebrews exhorts us to "Look unto Jesus the author and finisher of our faith" (Hebrews 12:2). "Let us hold fast the profession of our faith without wavering; for He is faithful that promised" (Hebrews 10:23). The promise is that we are "blessed and holy" when we have part in the first resurrection (Revelation 20:6).

The Lord Jesus Christ has become the supreme symbol of faith in all of biblical history. Humanity's greatest adventure will be that of gaining eternal life. The final symbol of faith is Jesus Christ. God has used many symbols of faith throughout the scriptures of which I have cited just a few. However, there is no symbol as great as the Lord Jesus Christ. For it is through Christ that we have the wonderful privilege of becoming Sons of the living God. It is through this magnificent symbol of faith that we will be changed from corruptible to incorruptible; from mortal to immortality (1st Corinthian 15:54) HALLELUJAH!!!

Symbols of Faith and the Miracles of God

The greatest miracle stemming from the greatest symbol of faith is the resurrection. It is greater than the creation of the sun, moon, and stars. It is greater than the sea and all the fish in the sea. The miracle of the resurrection is greater than all the creations of God combined. I say that because death comes to everything. Death is final. When a loved one dies, we have that sense of finality; unless we have a hope of the resurrection. The fish does not come back to life when it dies. The animals do not come back to life when they die. Man is the only being that has the hope to be resurrected. Jesus Christ our great symbol of faith went to the cross and died. He was buried for three days and three nights. He was resurrected the third day without a trace of corruption as was prophesied of Him in Psalm 16:8-10:

> *I have set the Lord always before me because*
> *He is at my right hand I shall not be moved. Therefore*
> *my heart is glad and my glory rejoices; my flesh also shall*
> *rest in hope for thou wilt not leave my soul in hell,*
> *neither wilt thou suffer thy holy one to see corruption.*

No, death is not final for man. The only requirement is that man will see the great symbol of faith, Jesus Christ, which God has given unto us. The only requirement is that man accepts God's symbol of faith and allow Jesus Christ to transform his life. This transformation produces a change from sin to righteousness, from death to eternal life. The benefits are that after the resurrection there will be no death. There will be no pain. There will be no disappointments. Those that are transformed and built into the church that Jesus is building will live a life of luxury with responsibility. They will have a mansion that is paid for, and where the streets are paved with gold (St. John 14:21: Revelation 21:21). The resurrection gives eternal life, and that life is filled with eternal happiness. Eternal life is filled with eternal joy. Every day is a good day. The resurrection gives us an environment that is free from rain, snow, sleet, and ice storms. Pollution will be non-existent. Resurrection life is always glorious.

My friend, now that you have read this book and you know that you do not have a right relationship with our Lord Jesus Christ, the greatest symbol of faith of all times, I strongly urge you to humble yourself right now and repent of your sins to God. Remember that physical death is not the end of all life. There will be a resurrection of the dead. Jesus gave us the assurance of the resurrection when He rose from the dead after three days and three nights in the grave. The first resurrection insures a life filled with eternal happiness.

I pray for God's eternal blessings for you and I do hope that you have gained useful spiritual insights in the recognition of the symbols of faith recorded in the Bible. As you read and study the Bible, look for other symbols of faith. Learn to create your own so that you can receive mighty miracles from the greatest symbol of faith, The Lord Jesus Christ.

Conclusion

The purpose of this book is to help fellow believers in Christ and all who read, more readily recognize the great symbols of faith that produces the great miracles that are in the Bible.

My hope is that you will be enlightened as you walk through these wonderful symbols. I highlighted the burning bush symbol, the rock in the wilderness symbol, the hem of His garment symbol and a few others with the hope that you will become anointed to do your own research to find other symbols of faith that may bless your soul and move you to a higher dimension of faith. The greater the faith you have in God, the more magnificent the miracles you will receive and experience.

Some of the symbols of faith that have blessed me that I have not included in the book are the River Jordan for the Syrian Naaman and Esther's banquet for the King that saved the Jews from certain death. My friend be a true worshiper.

Thank you so very much for reading this book.

Endnotes:

[1] Exodus 3:1-4
[2] Hebrews 11:6
[3] Exodus 3:11, 4:1,10
[4] II Corinthians 5:7
[5] Acts 9:3-5
[6] Exodus 3:4, Acts 9:4
[7] Exodus 3:13-14
[8] Acts 9:5
[9] Exodus 4:1-2
[10] Romans 12:1
[11] Exodus 4: 1-8
[12] Exodus 4:8
[13] Romans 10:17
[14] Exodus 5:28-31
[15] Exodus 7:9-12
[16] Exodus 14:16
[17] Exodus 14:28-29
[18] I John 5:4
[19] Genesis 15:25
[20] Exodus 15: 22-26
[21] I Thessalonians 5:18
[22] Exodus 17
[23] Hebrew 1 (amp)
[24] Mark 11:23
[25] Hebrews 4:16
[26] Exodus 31:18
[27] Deuteronomy 6:4
[28] http://aboutfood.org/almonds.htm
[29] Hebrews 11:6
[30] I Kings 17:9
[31] Luke 4:22-26
[32] I Kings 17: 14-15
[33] 1Kings 19:21
[34] John 6:5
[35] John 6:7

Order Form

To place an order, please fill out the form in its entirety.

Name:_____

Address:_____

City, State, Zip Code:_____

Quantity:_____

Price:___$17.95_____

Shipping:

_____1st Class U.S. Mail _____Overnight,

_____2nd day   _____3rd day

(additional charges will apply)

Mail to:

Wells of Water Publishing

Post Office Box 47335

Windsor Mill, Maryland 21244

Allow 2-3 weeks for delivery

110